The Information Age

Other books in the Current Controversies series:

The Information Age

James D. Torr, *Book Editor*

Daniel Leone, *President*
Bonnie Szumski, *Publisher*
Scott Barbour, *Managing Editor*

CURRENT CONTROVERSIES

GREENHAVEN
PRESS®

THOMSON
———*———
™
GALE

San Diego • Detroit • New York • San Francisco • Cleveland
New Haven, Conn. • Waterville, Maine • London • Munich

12/02

LIBRARY OF CONGRESS CATALOGING-IN-PUBLICATION DATA

The information age / James D. Torr, book editor.
  p. cm. — (Current controversies)
Includes bibliographical references and index.
ISBN 0-7377-1186-8 (lib. bdg. : alk. paper) — ISBN 0-7377-1185-X (pbk. : alk. paper)
  1. Information society. 2. Information technology—Social aspects. I. Torr,
James D., 1974– . II. Series.
HM851 .I528 2003
303.48'33—dc21   2002066821

Printed in the United States of America

Contents

nology has made the economy more robust and productive than ever
before and will continue to do so in the foreseeable future.

No: The Information Age Has Not Created a New Economy

Chapter 3: How Should Governments Respond to the Information Age?

The Government Should Regulate Information Technology

Foreword

By definition, controversies are "discussions of questions in which opposing opinions clash" (Webster's Twentieth Century Dictionary Unabridged). Few would deny that controversies are a pervasive part of the human condition and exist on virtually every level of human enterprise. Controversies transpire between individuals and among groups, within nations and between nations. Controversies supply the grist necessary for progress by providing challenges and challengers to the status quo. They also create atmospheres where strife and warfare can flourish. A world without controversies would be a peaceful world; but it also would be, by and large, static and prosaic.

The Series' Purpose

The purpose of the Current Controversies series is to explore many of the social, political, and economic controversies dominating the national and international scenes today. Titles selected for inclusion in the series are highly focused and specific. For example, from the larger category of criminal justice, Current Controversies deals with specific topics such as police brutality, gun control, white collar crime, and others. The debates in Current Controversies also are presented in a useful, timeless fashion. Articles and book excerpts included in each title are selected if they contribute valuable, long-range ideas to the overall debate. And wherever possible, current information is enhanced with historical documents and other relevant materials. Thus, while individual titles are current in focus, every effort is made to ensure that they will not become quickly outdated. Books in the Current Controversies series will remain important resources for librarians, teachers, and students for many years.

In addition to keeping the titles focused and specific, great care is taken in the editorial format of each book in the series. Book introductions and chapter prefaces are offered to provide background material for readers. Chapters are organized around several key questions that are answered with diverse opinions representing all points on the political spectrum. Materials in each chapter include opinions in which authors clearly disagree as well as alternative opinions in which authors may agree on a broader issue but disagree on the possible solutions. In this way, the content of each volume in Current Controversies mirrors the mosaic of opinions encountered in society. Readers will quickly realize that there are many viable answers to these complex issues. By questioning each author's conclusions, students and casual readers can begin to develop the critical thinking skills so important to evaluating opinionated material.

Current Controversies is also ideal for controlled research. Each anthology in the series is composed of primary sources taken from a wide gamut of informational categories including periodicals, newspapers, books, United States and foreign government documents, and the publications of private and public organizations. Readers will find factual support for reports, debates, and research papers covering all areas of important issues. In addition, an annotated table of contents, an index, a book and periodical bibliography, and a list of organizations to contact are included in each book to expedite further research.

Perhaps more than ever before in history, people are confronted with diverse and contradictory information. During the Persian Gulf War, for example, the public was not only treated to minute-to-minute coverage of the war, it was also inundated with critiques of the coverage and countless analyses of the factors motivating U.S. involvement. Being able to sort through the plethora of opinions accompanying today's major issues, and to draw one's own conclusions, can be a complicated and frustrating struggle. It is the editors' hope that Current Controversies will help readers with this struggle.

Greenhaven Press anthologies primarily consist of previously published material taken from a variety of sources, including periodicals, books, scholarly journals, newspapers, government documents, and position papers from private and public organizations. These original sources are often edited for length and to ensure their accessibility for a young adult audience. The anthology editors also change the original titles of these works in order to clearly present the main thesis of each viewpoint and to explicitly indicate the opinion presented in the viewpoint. These alterations are made in consideration of both the reading and comprehension levels of a young adult audience. Every effort is made to ensure that Greenhaven Press accurately reflects the original intent of the authors included in this anthology.

"The new century will be dominated by the transformation in the cost of transporting knowledge and ideas."

Introduction

Technology has the power to transform society. The most famous example of this is German craftsman Johannes Gutenberg's invention of the printing press in the fifteenth century. *Washington Post* columnist Robert J. Samuelson sums up the vast changes that occurred as a result of the invention of printing: "Gutenberg's press led to mass literacy, fostered the Protestant Reformation (by undermining the clergy's theological monopoly) and, through the easy exchange of information, enabled the scientific revolution." Subsequent technological advances are also often evaluated in terms of the effect they had on society. James Watt's steam engine, for example, is often credited with starting the Industrial Revolution in England. Today, the Internet and associated information technologies are said to be behind an information revolution that is transforming the way people live and work.

Unlike the printing press or the steam engine, no single person invented the Internet. Instead it was the culmination of advances in computer technology, reductions in the cost of manufacturing personal computers and the resulting increase in their popularity, and the evolution of networking technology.

The Internet is essentially a vast network of computers. Importantly, it is a decentralized network; it does not depend on a central mainframe computer as networks did in the 1950s and 1960s. The idea for a vast, decentralized computer network originated with the Cold War and the U.S. Department of Defense's Advanced Research Projects Agency (ARPA). ARPA scientists and engineers wanted to create a computer network in which any computer could exchange information with any other computer. The destruction of one or more parts of the network—perhaps from a Soviet attack—would not disrupt communication between other computers in the system.

Computers were first linked to form ARPANET, as this early network was called, in 1969. Throughout the 1970s and 1980s, as computers became more common, academic researchers and engineers began linking their computers to ARPANET. As the network grew—branching haphazardly and quite beyond the control of its original creators—it came to be known as the "Internet."

Many people associate the Internet with e-mail. E-mail is only one of the many ways that information can be shared over the Internet, but e-mail was one of the most popular uses for the Internet in its early years. Researchers welcomed e-mail as a fast, easy, and free way to communicate with colleagues. Researchers also experimented with different ways of transporting files across the Internet.

In order to share computer files across the Internet, the computers on the network need to share a common protocol, or standard, for how the data will be transported electronically. The most famous such protocol—and the one that propelled the Internet to nationwide popularity—is Hypertext Markup Language, or HTML. HTML was invented by Tim Berners-Lee, a British computer programmer who developed the protocol as a convenient way of sharing documents over the Internet. In 1991 HTML became the basis for the World Wide Web, a subset of the Internet in which HTML documents are grouped to form websites that are linked to one another.

The World Wide Web made the Internet more easily accessible and for many people, fun to use. Instead of just text, Internet users could now access still pictures, animation, and sound. As a result, the Internet experienced an enormous surge in popularity throughout the 1990s. Whereas in 1993 there were less than 90,000 people using the Internet on a regular basis, in 1999 there were approximately 171 million, and in 2000 there were over 300 million. Estimates in 2001 indicate that 58 percent of the U.S. population, or 165.18 million people, have access to the Internet at home. Government and independent market research indicates that the number of Internet users could reach 1 billion by 2005.

The phenomenal growth of the Internet is a major component of the information revolution, but it is not the only part. The Internet has spurred a wave of innovation in communications technology. Not just computers, but also cell phones, personal digital assistants, and even automobiles can now link to the Internet. And software companies have developed countless applications to harness the Internet's potential.

Many of these applications are business-oriented. The instantaneous access to information that the Internet offers has revolutionized the way many companies do business. It has also given rise to a new type of business: e-commerce. E-retailers like Amazon.com essentially offer customers a convenient, interactive, customizable, and constantly updated mail-order catalog, while others, such as the auction site eBay, offer services that would not be possible without the World Wide Web. E-commerce generated almost $47.6 billion in revenue in 2001.

Investors will continue to monitor the Internet's effect on the economy, but the social aspects of the Information Revolution—its effects on everything from entertainment to education to government—are harder to quantify. Many commentators question just how sweeping the changes wrought by information technology have been. Others wonder whether those changes are on par with the societal transformations brought on by past technologies such as the printing press and the steam engine. Robert J. Samuelson believes it may be too soon to judge the impact of new information technologies: "Technologies acquire historical weight by reshaping the human condition," he writes. "As yet the Internet isn't in the same league with [past] developments." Frances Cairncross, the author of *The Death of Distance: How the Communications Revolution Is Changing Our Lives*, makes a bolder prediction:

> Think of [the information revolution] as one of the three great revolutions in the cost of transport. The nineteenth century, dominated by the steamship and the railway, saw a transformation in the cost of transporting goods; the twentieth century, with first the motor car and then the aeroplane, in the cost of transporting people. The new century will be dominated by the transformation in the cost of transporting knowledge and ideas.

The authors in *Current Controversies: The Information Age* explore the issues raised by information technology in the following chapters: How Has the Information Age Affected Society? Has the Information Age Created a New Economy? How Should Governments Respond to the Information Age? What Is the Future of the Information Age? The authors in this volume seek to provide insight into the impact of information technology on society. This is a formidable task, since the Information Age is itself characterized by constant change. As Cairncross notes, "That these technologies will change the world is beyond a doubt. The way that they will do so is more mysterious."

Chapter 1

How Has the Information Age Affected Society?

Chapter Preface

Computers, the Internet, and other information technologies are extraordinarily powerful tools. As such they have great potential both to benefit and to harm societies that embrace them. For example, the Internet has been used to make businesses more efficient, improve education, and create online meeting places for people separated by great distances; it has also produced a new avenue for fraud, theft, invasion of privacy, and the distribution of pornography and hate speech.

The September 11, 2001, terrorist attacks on the World Trade Center and the Pentagon were an example of the Internet's power as a tool for both good and evil. A few weeks after September 11, *Yahoo! Internet Life* reported that although the terrorists used only knives and boxcutters to execute the attacks, "The World Trade Center attack, a morbid masterpiece whose perfect execution required both intricate and covert coordination, simply would not have been possible without the Internet. Every aspect of the planning of this horrific event bore the marks of the information revolution." The FBI has reported that terrorist leader Osama bin Laden has used the Internet to spread propaganda and recruit troops. The anonymity of the Internet makes it an appealing communications network for criminals, and advances in encryption technology have made it much harder for law enforcement agencies to monitor suspected terrorists.

On the other hand, information technology also played a positive role on September 11, helping the nation come together in a time of crisis. The Internet has its roots in the U.S. military's plans for a decentralized communications network that could withstand an enemy attack on North America. If part of the system was damaged, messages would be rerouted and still reach their destinations. This is exactly how e-mail worked on the day of the attacks. "From a purely technical perspective," explains Massachusetts Institute of Technology professor Henry Jenkins, "the system worked better than anyone might have anticipated. While the World Trade Center housed an important relay system for cell phones, and its destruction thus left many New Yorkers without telecommunications, there was no significant national disruption of the computer networks." Countless e-mails were sent from New York City when telephone services were disrupted in the area. And across the country, people used the Internet to seek information about friends and family they could not reach by phone.

The September 11 terrorist attacks serve as a reminder of how much Americans have come to depend on the Internet, and how the technology can be misused. In the following chapter, authors debate whether the advances of the Information Age have benefited or harmed society.

The Internet Benefits Society

by W. David Stephenson

About the author: *W. David Stephenson is an Internet strategist and futurist. He teaches Internet strategy courses at Bentley College in Waltham, Massachusetts.*

Now that legions of Internet workers—including me—are unemployed, I'm frequently asked about the Internet's future.

True, maybe people aren't as eager to buy dog food or patio furniture online as we may have thought a year ago. But the Internet's impact remains profound—and highly beneficial. Three positive principles fostered by the Internet have altered the way we live and do business: linking everything, closing the loop, and empowering individuals.

Linking everything: When the Defense Department launched ARPANET, the Internet's precursor, in 1969, the government made a conscious decision not to set rules for its use. Rather, rules evolved through a collaborative effort by users in government, academia, and corporations. Today, that spirit of cooperation and the ease of linkage the Web allows are altering competition and society.

Early in the 1990s, cheap Russian imports threatened Boeing's Rocketdyne engine unit. Boeing responded by making its design process for engines collaborative. Previously, its engineers designed the engines, then turned them over to suppliers, who made the parts. Today, Rocketdyne's "extranet"—a portion of their intranet that's available by password to authorized outsiders—involves suppliers throughout the design process.

Team members work concurrently instead of sequentially, and everyone has access to relevant information.

The payoffs for Rocketdyne are astonishing: Prototype costs were cut from $1.4 million to only $50,000, the number of parts in an engine went from 140 to five, and design time was cut from seven person years to less than one.

Linking information is just as important as linking people. As Tim Berners-Lee, the World Wide Web's father, wrote, "The dream behind the Web is of a common information space in which we communicate by sharing information."

Charles Vest, president of the Massachusetts Institute of Technology, captured that spirit in his announcement [in April 2001] that the university would make most course content available—for free—on the Web: "It expresses our belief in the way education can be advanced by constantly widening access to information and by inspiring others to participate."

The Web of Ideas

I suspect the Internet's most fundamental contribution to progress may be this ability to link ideas formerly isolated from one another. That will facilitate inclusive solutions to complex issues that would be impossible with piecemeal approaches.

Closing the loop: The Internet is truly a web that makes it as easy to respond as to initiate. That contrasts with the old "linear fashion" of working and governing, when feedback by users of a product or citizens affected by a government program rarely reached those creating the goods and services.

Now it is easy to feed back information and make quick revisions. For example, in Massachusetts, the company Systems Engineering Inc. designed a website with linkages that allows social workers to track and coordinate all the relevant services available to help at-risk youths, and then monitor their progress and fine tune the combination of services.

> *"The Internet's impact remains profound—and highly beneficial."*

Similarly, Adobe software designers don't guess what customers might want in upgrades. They simply monitor their "user to user" forums to learn about real-life problems that can't be anticipated in the lab.

Empowering the individual: One student, Sean Fanning, brought the music industry to its knees when he leveraged that empowerment to share music with friends. Mr. Fanning's product, Napster—a free system for downloading and sharing music via the Internet—is on the legal ropes, but the industry's victory is Pyrrhic.

Other new Web-based systems facilitate sharing without needing a single website, which is vulnerable to lawsuits.

Xerox Corp. saves millions in repair costs by using a knowledge-management system, Eureka, which works because it gives individual workers power to contribute to it. Originally resisted by senior management, Eureka lets field service people contribute their own solutions to real-world problems to a database that's instantly available to their peers.

Field rep Chuck Rutkowski told *Darwin Magazine* that he uses Eureka daily because the information comes from his counterparts: "If I want to know what temperature the water is, I'm going to ask the guys splashing around in the water, not the guy standing on shore."

18

Chapter 1

If the "irrational exuberance" about the Internet has been dashed, that's not all bad. Maybe the English language can be spared those abominable "e-" and "i-" words.

But I'd say a technology that can create a society and economy in which we are all interdependent, where "virtuous circles" speed beneficial change, and, most important, where individuals are valued and empowered, really does change everything—for the better.

The Information Age Has Improved Everyday Life

by Carter Henderson

About the author: *Carter Henderson is a writer who is completing a book on the impact of the Information Revolution on our daily lives.*

"Whether you sell stock or sell suits, the Internet has changed the world," says Richard A. Grasso, chairman of the New York Stock Exchange, and he couldn't be more on the money.

Today, there's scarcely an aspect of our life that isn't being upended by the torrent of information available on the hundreds of millions of sites crowding the Internet, not to mention its ability to keep us in constant touch with each other via electronic mail. "If the automobile and aerospace technology had exploded at the same pace as computer and information technology," says Microsoft, "a new car would cost about $2 and go 600 miles on a thimble of gas. And you could buy a Boeing 747 for the cost of a pizza."

Probably the biggest payoff, however, is the billions of dollars the Internet is saving companies in producing goods and serving the needs of their customers. Nothing like it has been seen since the beginning of the Industrial Revolution, when power-driven machines began producing more in a day than men could turn out in nearly a year. "We view the growth of the Internet and e-commerce as a global megatrend," says Merrill Lynch, "along the lines of the printing press, the telephone, the computer, and electricity."

You would be hard pressed to name something that isn't available on the Internet. Consider: books, health care, movie tickets, construction materials, baby clothes, stocks, cattle feed, music, electronics, antiques, tools, real estate, toys, autographs of famous people, wine, pornography, and airline tickets. And even after you've moved on to your final resting place, there's no reason those you love can't keep in touch. A company called FinalThoughts.com offers a place for you to store "afterlife e-mails" you can send to Heaven with the help of a "guardian angel."

Excerpted from "How the Internet Is Changing Our Lives," by Carter Henderson, *Futurist*, July 2000. Copyright © 2000 by World Future Society. Reprinted with permission.

Kids today are so computer savvy that it virtually ensures the United States will remain the unchallenged leader in cyberspace for the foreseeable future. Nearly all children in families with incomes of more than $75,000 a year have home computers, according to a study by the David and Lucile Packard Foundation. Youngsters from ages 2 to 17 at all income levels have computers, with 52% of those connected to the Internet. Most kids use computers to play games (some for 30 hours or more a week), and many teenage girls think nothing of rushing home from school to have e-mail chats with friends they had just left.

What's clear is that, whether we like it or not, the Internet is an ever growing part of our lives and there is no turning back. "The Internet is just 20% invented," says cyber pioneer Jake Winebaum. "The last 80% is happening now." . . .

Vanishing Startups

IBM CEO Louis V. Gerstner Jr. calls the thousands of Internet startups that disappeared soon after their initial capital infusions ran out "fire flies before the storm." Their names are legion, and more have been rushing to join without letup. Garden.com (gardening supplies), Living.com (home furnishings), Toysmart.com (educational playthings), Eve.com (beauty products), Homewarehouse.com (household products), Cyberhomes (where prospective home buyers could access listings of properties for sale), Red Gorilla.com (online billing), Craftshop.com (arts and crafts store), and Babygear.com (discount baby products) are all illustrative of what Gerstner dubs "dot-toast."

> *"There's scarcely an aspect of our life that isn't being upended by the torrent of information available on . . . the Internet."*

Dot-coms have been failing at the same time as the number of online customers has been exploding. It's believed the Internet was born in 1969 when two computers at the University of California, Los Angeles, were connected by a 15-foot cable, with bits of meaningless data flowing between them. Since then the Net has taken off, with some 137 million U.S. computers online plus another 152 million outside the United States, according to the U.S. Internet Council in Washington, D.C. And while the number of Internet-linked computers is surging, the volume of traffic they are carrying is increasing even faster. Some projections have it doubling every 100 days.

This is not surprising since a hallmark of the Cyber Age is connectivity and the sharing of information. The assertion that "information is meant to be free" is an increasing reality since it can be moved from those who have it to those who need it in the blink of an eye—and at virtually no cost, unlike for other media. This computer-driven contribution to the vitality of the U.S. economy is immeasurable. . . .

Auction sites have been springing up all over the Internet, but the undisputed leader is eBay. Operating out of its sparkling headquarters in San Jose, California, eBay claims close to 13 million registered users on any given day. They place 1,000 bids a minute on some 4 million items put up for sale, from antiques to sports memorabilia.

You simply go to eBay's Web site, register, post a description of what you have to sell, along with photos and a minimum price, if you like. Bids from interested buyers appear on your computer screen, which is instantly updated as better bids come in. Once the auction ends, the highest bidder is obliged to pay for the item, usually with a money order or cashier's check, before the item is delivered. While most auction sites follow eBay's lead by starting off with the lowest bid, others such as Basement.com and OutletZoo.com start prices high and drop them little by little until the item is sold.

> *"The Internet is an ever growing part of our lives and there is no turning back."*

Americans spend more on entertainment than on clothing or health care, and the convergence of computers and telecommunications is generating new ways to amuse ourselves undreamed of until now.

Bring up the Web site of Computer Gaming World (CGW) magazine and you suddenly become a stranger in a strange land. Cyber versions of golden oldies such as tiddlywinks are nowhere to be found, and in their place are PC-powered Planescape: Torment; Tomb Raider: The Last Revolution; Final Fantasy VIII; and Abomination. . . .

Today's near runaway fascination with sex, reflected in the more than 40,000 lurid sites competing for business on the Internet, has thrown a spotlight on something that until recently was confined to the shadows. In the early to mid-1990s, up to 80% of all Internet traffic was adult related. Even today, the adult-entertainment industry still drives the Internet, with profit margins of 30% or more, even though they have no off-line revenue stream generated by magazines, books, videocassettes, etc. But in the past couple of years, cybersex has moved uptown: Among the four-star sex sites is Blowfish.com, which offers toys, books, videos, supplies, comics, magazines, and objets d'art designed for "your erotic enjoyment."

One of the Internet's truly great features is that anybody can be a player who has an idea for a Web site and a few dollars to get it up and running. Possibly the most notorious site of all is the one dreamed up by an 18-year-old dropout from Northeastern University in Boston, Shawn Fanning, nicknamed the "Napster" for his unruly red hair. He created the world's biggest online free-music community, which allows 38 million popular music lovers to swap hundreds of recordings, using the Napster system as a search engine to find exactly what they want.

Napster has outraged everyone connected with the record business, from artists whose creative work was being hijacked to the Recording Industry Association of America, which brought a lawsuit seeking an injunction aimed at ending Napster's brief, if notorious life. It now appears, incredibly, that this deadlock may actually be resolved to almost everyone's satisfaction. Napster users may pay a modest monthly fee, which will be divided up among those creating, producing, and delivering the music. Napster is receiving financial backing from the German media giant Bertelsmann, which is getting a piece of Napster in return. There is a sticking point, however, since it's now unclear how to put a user name and price on every digital music file being downloaded. It's also unclear if Napster users will pay even a few bucks a month for the service.

The Land of Free Stuff

Cyberspace is a veritable heaven for those looking for something for nothing— or nearly nothing. FreeStuff-Net.com provides access to an assortment of sites offering handouts. There's "Just Free Stuff," "Freebie Land," "It's Free 4U," "Planet Freebie," "Free Love," "Free Samples," and "Free.com." Beware—the goal of many such sites is simply to get your name and address. . . .

It would be unfair to leave the wonderful world of free stuff without mentioning Blue Mountain Arts Publishing, launched by two former hippies as a "spiritual and emotional center for the Web." Their stroke of genius was to give away billions of online greeting cards in nine different languages, absolutely free. This concept was so exciting that the owners of the Excite@Home Web site agreed to pay about $1 billion for the company if it met certain sales targets during the holidays when most greeting cards are sold.

But why would any serious business agree to give away so much stuff? The answer is that the bluemountain.com site gets about a million hits a day from people ordering free cards for dozens of occasions, and most of them also order flowers, candy, and gifts, which is where Excite@Home sees a potential gold mine. It's even introduced a new high-tech card that can be used to send loved ones electronic flowers.

Experts Online

From time to time, we need an expert. In such situations, the Internet has been like a gift from the gods. In the old days, authorities were near at hand for expert advice: the village seamstress on how to make a buttonhole, the blacksmith on how to take care of a horse's hooves, or the apothecary on what to do about warts. On the Internet, advice and answer sites are popping up all over the place, with self-proclaimed experts at the ready.

Exp.com claims to have "tens of thousands of experts who can help you," while the more restrained Abuzz.com, owned by *The New York Times,* limits its pitch to "Ask Anything! Real People. Real Answers." It's said that expert sites or knowledge networks represent the latest stage in the Internet's evolution, a "democratization of expertise." However, if your question is about something other than "Who invented the light bulb?" the answers are likely to be a wild potpourri of personal opinions.

Online Education

Top colleges and universities are rushing into online education, but the big news is the proliferation of a new breed of for-profit online institutions bringing Internet education to the masses. "The Internet will probably be the single most democratizing force in education," says Columbia Business School Dean Meyer Feldberg, who envisions educational programs being routed through the Net to hundreds of millions of people.

The largest online institution is the University of Phoenix (http://onl. uophx.edu/), with some 6,000 students today and hopes of reaching 200,000 students in 10 years. The University offers bachelor's, master's, and doctoral degrees in business management, technology, education, and nursing. The institution boasts that if you're a student "you can earn your degree via the Internet whenever and wherever you want." The University notes that its degree programs cost far less and may take some students far less time to complete.

On the other hand, a *Business Week* survey of 247 companies found that only a handful would consider hiring applicants who earned their MBA degrees online. Whether that will change as for-profit online universities improve their offerings—and graduates prove their worth—is anyone's guess. . . .

"Old" Economy Greets the "New"

Corporations have suddenly awakened to the fact that the Internet can save them billions of dollars in conducting their everyday affairs, with some of it showing up in lower prices for the consumer. And it's only the beginning. "Where do you think we are as an economy as far as e-business goes?" *Fortune* magazine recently asked General Electric's legendary CEO Jack Welch, who immediately replied, "First inning."

How right he is can be seen in a two-story brick building on Chicago's industrial South Side, home to the Corrugated Supplies Corporation, which manufactures corrugated sheets for boxes and other products. Despite the company's low-tech image, owner Rick Van Horne may have moved e-business into a second inning and then some: The computerized production system that he built by hand can fill customers' orders—to their exact specifications—and deliver the goods in less than 24 hours, with a 35% reduction in waste.

> *"One of the Internet's truly great features is that anybody can be a player who has an idea for a Web site and a few dollars to get it up and running."*

This success hiked Corrugated Supplies' sales from $40 million in 1997 to $100 million in 2000. Van Horne is now offering to teach other companies everything he knows about building high-tech factories.

The billions of dollars a year that American companies are saving thanks to the Internet's ability to slash their cost of doing business is making them even more successful competitors on world markets. This is reflected in better prices for their customers and increased profits for themselves, with much of it coming from greatly improved ways of cutting costs.

Ford, General Motors, and DaimlerChrysler, among others, have created Covisint, a $300-billion mega market for buying auto parts. It's a new world out there, with companies large and small banding together to force suppliers to trim their prices or lose the business. Still others are doing this on their own, such as the big air-conditioner parts manufacturer Trane Company, which set up its own private online exchange that forced its 5,000 dealers to continually bid against each other for its business.

Where Do We Go Next?

The rest of the world is moving into cyberspace more slowly than the United States, and, in the developing world, the Internet has hardly penetrated at all. U.N. Secretary-General Kofi Annan is determined to change this through the United Nations Information Technology Service, which will train large numbers of people to tap into the income enhancing power of the Internet. Annan is also proposing an Internet health network that will provide state-of-the-art medical knowledge to 10,000 clinics and hospitals in poor countries.

The onrushing Cyber Age has given newfound power to us all, as seen in Jody Williams's one-woman organization using e-mail to promote a global ban on land mines. Yet, this is but a glimpse of what's ahead in the minds of those immersed in this great and accelerating transformation.

The Internet Fosters Online Communities

by John B. Horrigan

About the author: *John B. Horrigan is a senior researcher at the Pew Internet & American Life Project, an initiative of the Pew Research Center that studies the Internet's growth and societal impact.*

In recent years, there has been concern about the social impact of the Internet on several levels. One major worry was that use of the Internet would prompt people to withdraw from social engagement and become isolated, depressed, and alienated. A related fear was that Internet users might abandon contact with their local communities as they discovered how easy it is to go online to communicate with those in other parts of the world and get information from every point on the planet.

We surveyed 1,697 Internet users in January and February [2001] to explore the breadth and depth of community online. Our findings suggest that the online world is a vibrant social universe where many Internet users enjoy serious and satisfying contact with online communities. These online groups are made up of those who share passions, beliefs, hobbies, or lifestyles. Tens of millions of Americans have joined communities after discovering them online. And many are using the Internet to join and participate in longstanding, traditional groups such as professional and trade associations. All in all, 84% of Internet users have at one time or another contacted an online group.

The pull of online communities in the aftermath of the September 11 attacks shows how Americans have integrated online communities into their lives. In the days following the attacks, 33% of American Internet users read or posted material in chat rooms, bulletin boards, or other online forums. Although many early posts reflected outrage at the events, online discussions soon migrated to grieving, discussion and debate on how to respond, and information queries about the suspects and those who sponsored them. With the dramatic displays of community spirit around the country following September 11, there are hopes that

Americans' repulsion and shock [concerning] the attacks might have sparked a renewal of civic spirit in the United States. The existing vibrancy of online communities profiled in this report suggests that Internet groups can play a supporting role in any enduring boon to community life in the aftermath of the attacks.

Our winter survey also showed that many Americans are using the Internet to intensify their connection to their local community. They employ email to plan church meetings, arrange neighborhood gatherings, and petition local politicians. They use the Web to find out about local merchants, get community news, and check out area fraternal organizations. Moreover, there is evidence that this kind of community engagement is particularly appealing to young adults.

"Glocalization"

Sociologist Barry Wellman argues that many new social arrangements are being formed through "glocalization"—the capacity of the Internet to expand users' social worlds to faraway people and simultaneously to bind them more deeply to the place where they live.

This report illustrates how widely "glocalization" is occurring. The Internet helps many people find others who share their interests no matter how distant they are, and it also helps them increase their contact with groups and people they already know and it helps them feel more connected to them.

90 million Americans have participated in online groups:

- 84% of Internet users, or about 90 million Americans, say they have used the Internet to contact or get information from a group. We call them "Cyber Groupies."
- 79% of Cyber Groupies identify at least one particular group with which they stay in regular contact.
- 49% of Cyber Groupies say the Internet has helped them connect with groups or people who share their interests.
- Cyber Groupies try out different groups; the average Cyber Groupie has contacted four online groups at one time or another.

Use of the Internet often prompts Americans to join groups. More than half of Cyber Groupies (56%) say they joined an online group *after* they began communicating with it over the Internet. This includes those who joined traditional groups whose existence predated the Internet, such as

> *"The online world is a vibrant social universe where many Internet users enjoy serious and satisfying contact with online communities."*

professional or fraternal groups. In other words, Internet access is helping people join all kinds of communities, including those that are not exclusively virtual communities.

- 40% of Cyber Groupies say the Internet has helped them become more involved with groups to which they already belong.

In addition to helping users participate in communities of interest that often have no geographical boundaries, the Internet is a tool for those who are involved with local groups, particularly church groups.

- 26% of Internet users have employed the Internet to contact or get information about local groups. That comes to 28 million people.

Virtual Third Places

In the face of widespread worries that community activity is ebbing in the United States, these findings demonstrate that the Internet, while not necessarily turning the tide, has become an important new tool to connect people with shared interests globally and locally. In some ways, online communities have become *virtual third places* for people because they are different places from home and work. These places allow people either to hang out with others or more actively engage with professional associations, hobby groups, religious organizations, or sports leagues.

> *"Internet access is helping people join all kinds of communities, including those that are not exclusively virtual communities."*

These groups are lively online communities. People exchange emails, hash out issues, find out about group activities, and meet face-to-face as a result of online communities. Approximately 23 million Americans are *very* active in online communities, meaning that they email their principle online group several times a week.

- 60% of Cyber Groupies say they use email to communicate with the group; of these emailers, 43% email the group several times a week.
- 33% of the 28 million Local Groupies who use email send email to their main local organization several times a week.

Many Cyber Groupies and Local Groupies say that online communities have spurred connections to strangers and to people of different racial, ethnic, and economic backgrounds.

- 50% of Cyber Groupies say that participation in an online community has helped them get to know people they otherwise would not have met.
- 35% of Local Groupies say that participation in an online community has helped them get to know people they otherwise would not have met. This lower number relative to Cyber Groupies may be due to the fact that Local Groupies probably were acquainted already with members of the online group.
- 37% of Cyber Groupies say the Internet has helped them connect with people of different ages or generations.
- 27% of Cyber Groupies say the Internet has helped them connect with people from different racial, ethnic, or economic backgrounds.

The types of connections people establish depend on the kind of group to which they belong. Members of some cyber groups go to their groups to establish personal relationships, while others just want to keep up with group news and activities.

- Members of belief groups, ethnic online groups, and especially online groups oriented to lifestyle issues are most interested in using the Internet to establish personal relationships.
- Members of entertainment, professional, and sports online groups tend to use email in group activities less often than those who belong to other kinds. They focus their online activities on getting information about popular culture.
- Men tend to be drawn to online groups involving professional activities, politics, and sports.
- Women tend to be drawn to online medical support groups, local community associations that are online, and cyber groups relating to entertainment.

There are differences between those who have used the Internet to join a group and those who use the Internet to participate in groups to which they already belong. Many who join online groups are relative newcomers to the Internet. They tend to be urban dwellers, young adults, and less well-educated than the typical Internet user. As a cohort they are more ethnically diverse than other Internet users, and more likely to be interested in online groups relating to fun activities.

The 56% of Cyber Groupies who joined a group after having first contacted it through the Internet have very different tastes in online groups than the "Long-timers" who belonged to the group before engaging with it online. Joiners of Cyber Groups identify hobby groups as the online community that they contact most, followed closely by trade or professional associations. A significant number of joiners also say they contact an online fan group of an entertainer or TV show. In contrast, Long-timers are most likely to say they are most closely in touch with trade or professional groups online.

At the local level, Long-timers are anchored in faith-based and community groups, while the joiners—who make up 20% of the Local Groupie population—show a greater tendency toward groups devoted to sports or with an explicitly social orientation.

Net Joiners of local groups are demographically diverse. They also tend to be highly experienced Internet users. This suggests that the Internet use is drawing new and different kinds of people to local groups. Once people have found local groups online and joined them, they report high levels of community involvement.

Civic Involvement by the Young

These differences among Joiners—particularly their relative youth, newness to the Internet, and racial diversity—suggests that the Internet may be drawing a segment of the population to community engagement who have not been very tied to civic activities. Political scientist Robert Putnam has argued that one major reason for the decline in civic engagement in the United States is the reluctance among younger people to participate in community groups. Our findings indicate that many young people are turning to the Internet as an outlet for community activity. Although young people tend to focus on online groups

> *"Online communities have spurred connections to strangers and to people of different racial, ethnic, and economic backgrounds."*

that involve hobbies, they also are much more likely than other users to report that the Internet has helped them become more involved with organizations in their community and connect with people of different generations, economic backgrounds, and ethnic groups. In other words, the primary draw to online communities for young people appears to be hobby groups; however, a secondary outcome, as young people surf to other online communities, is to connect many to groups that help foster civic engagement.

At the local level, people use the Internet mainly as an information utility to find out about local merchants and community activities. The Internet's role in public deliberation is modest. Public access to the Internet is only moderately available throughout the United States.

- 41% of Internet users say that they "often" or "sometimes" go online to seek out information about local stores or merchants.
- 35% of Internet users "often" or "sometimes" go online for news about their local community or to find out about community events.
- 30% go online "often" or "sometimes" for information about local government.
- 24% go online "often" or "sometimes" to get information about local schools.
- 13% of Internet users say that they "often" or "sometimes" email public officials. This low rate may be because only half of all Internet users say their town has a Web site, and few Internet users find the town's Web site very useful.
- 11% of Internet users say that they are aware of at least one local issue in which the Internet played a role in organizing citizens to communicate with public officials. However, this percentage doubles to 22% for Internet users who are active members of online communities.
- 51% of all Americans know of a place in their community where the Internet is publicly available. Overwhelmingly, these places are public libraries. African-Americans are the most likely to say that their community lacks public access to the Internet; 42% of African-Americans say their community does not have publicly available Internet terminals somewhere, compared with 29% of whites and 33% of Hispanics.

The Information Age Is Fostering the Spread of Freedom and Democracy

by Gary W. Selnow

About the author: *Gary W. Selnow is a professor of communication at San Francisco State University and executive director of WiRED (World Internet Resources for Education and Development), a nonprofit corporation that provides information and communication resources to disadvantaged groups around the world.*

[In 1997] we had the idea to install a few computers near Vukovar, Croatia to connect people to the Internet. Vukovar was hit hard during the [Balkan] wars, but it was not alone. Many other towns throughout the region were without libraries, news outlets, decent phone service or even mail delivery. Teachers were losing touch with developments in their fields, while professionals were falling behind their overseas colleagues, and average people were losing contact with loved ones who had scattered during the wars. The Internet offered a ready, high-tech answer to some very basic human needs.

Now fast forward to an Internet Center in Kosovo in the early summer of 2000. We had just finished the lecture portion of a training program for doctors, and the group was logging onto medical sites for a first look at the Web. They were using equipment provided by the American government through the Kosovo Internet Access Initiative. The physicians were strangely silent as they scrolled through the Web pages of the American Medical Association and the Centers for Disease Control. I had expected "oohs" and "aahs," not silence, and asked one of the doctors why everyone was quiet.

He said he and his colleagues were stunned. They had no idea that this was possible—that so much information could be delivered here to Pristina at the touch of a few keys. He could not believe they could retrieve in an instant information they had been without for so long. Soon, the doctors were filling floppy disks with articles and medical information like teenagers downloading Napster files. Apart from the immediate value of the information, can you imagine the impact of this experience on the doctors' perceptions of other societies where so much information is open to anyone, simply for the taking?

Preparing the World for Democracy

This is one example of how the Internet delivers much more than information. I don't want to overstate this, but we're seeing evidence that the Internet can play a significant role in preparing people for the transition to democracy. The Net is open, it links people across borders, it showcases life beyond the edge of town—and that feeds a process that prepares people for an open and civil society.

For too many years, the people in the Balkans have been the pawns of government. Now, they must prepare to run the game themselves. This is especially true for Serbia, which has just taken a big step into the future by sending Slobodan Milosevic off to the Hague for trial. Running their own government demands that people know the virtues of self-rule, the benefits of personal choice and the opportunities available to people who are free to direct their own lives.

Democracy in the Balkans, as elsewhere, is about a lot more than one-person-one-vote and free and fair elections. This became clear to me during the research and writing of a recent book on the politics and the press of Croatia. In addition to a free press and honest leaders, the people themselves must demand democracy. They have to seek it and grasp it—and if they don't, democracy cannot take hold.

U.S. Supreme Court Justice Louis Brandeis once wrote, "The greatest menace to freedom is an inert people." In Croatia, with a few exceptions during the past decade, the people had not demanded media access to government, even-handed coverage of political campaigns or a greater public role in governance. Thankfully, that changed some with last year's round of elections that swept the opposition into power, and now everyone anxiously watches Zagreb for the payoff of those extraordinary events.

Vaclav Havel, President of the Czech Republic—a man with some experience in cultivating an open government—zeroed in on the role of the public in the growth of democracy. Havel says that the people must feel democracy in their souls. He explains that spirit has to precede politics, ideas have to precede action, common sense and

> *"The Internet can play a significant role in preparing people for the transition to democracy."*

discussion have to precede political decisions. In other words, heart, mind and soul have to precede the political system. The human spirit has to be readied, or the mechanics of democracy—the campaigns, the reporting, the voting, the honest declaration of winners and losers—would become hollow pastimes.

Chapter 1

An Interactive Medium

Here is where I think the Internet stakes its claim. The most obvious features of the Net parallel traditional media. Like print, the Internet provides public information. Like the telephone, it permits interpersonal exchange. Like books and manuals, it offers tutorials. And like movies and TV, it provides entertainment. The Internet is a remarkable Swiss Army knife of information and communication, and unlike the other media, it does the job simultaneously in text, images, audio and video.

But the Net has unique features unknown to traditional media—feedback and interactivity. These are the keys to the personalization of communication. The real promise of the Net for democracy building is how people use it. Unlike the traditional one-way flow of information where audiences remain passive receptacles, the Internet gives users an active role as it enables them to fulfill personal requests. It provides a sense of control, and its user-driven choices reinforce this medium as a metaphor for self-determination. It is within the very nature of this use that I believe the Net can cultivate the soul of democracy. Let me give you a few examples.

Earlier I described the astonishment of physicians who logged onto the Internet for the first time. We witnessed similar reactions among engineers, attorneys and journalists who also got on the Net for the first time. What did they think as they pulled in

> *"Unlike the traditional one-way flow of information where audiences remain passive receptacles, the Internet gives users an active role."*

facts and statistics that had been out of their reach for so long? What did it say to them about places beyond their borders that could so freely create and maintain such volumes of information?

I wish you could have seen the 15-year-old Kosovar girl who asked if I could help her find a cousin who had fled before the war. The two best friends hadn't heard from each other in nearly two years. A Web search turned up a possibility in London, and the teenager emailed a message, hoping this note-in-a-cyber-bottle would find the girl she sought. The next day, she logged onto her Hotmail account and screeched at the sight of the "You Have Mail" message from her cousin. Before I left, she asked me to take her picture with my digital camera. Then she emailed it to London. A 15-year-old looks much different from the 13-year-old she was, and she wanted her cousin to notice.

What do you think this email episode said to these kids about a free exchange of information and about an open society? What do you think the Internet says to other teens in Kosovo who spend hours examining the Web sites of universities in the West? Our studies show that university searches are among the most popular activities for teens in Kosovo. What do you think it says about an open society to students who download newspaper articles, to pregnant women who obtain guidance about prenatal care, to disabled people who receive information about their disability and who communicate with others, thousands of miles away, who share their affliction?

The Power of the Internet

The cumulative effects of these experiences, I think, go a long way to preparing the soul for democracy. Since early spring of last year, among the seven Centers in Kosovo, we have recorded 750,000 online sessions.

I'd like to tell you another story about the power of the Internet in this region, and it begins with a six-year-old boy who had a hole in his heart. About a year ago, I was taking a van from Pristina to Skopje for a flight to the United States. Riding in the back seat was a frail kid whose fingernails were blue. A nurse was with him. She told me that a group in France had arranged to fly the boy to Paris where a volunteer team of doctors was standing by to repair his heart. The boy would remain in care for a month before returning to Kosovo.

His parents were poor and they had no funds for the journey. The nurse would leave him in Skopje. After that, the boy would be with strangers. And worse, the nurse told me there was a good chance that nobody at the hospital in France could speak Albanian. We can only imagine the horror that would tear through the mind of a six-year-old in a strange place, preparing for open-heart surgery without the reassurance of family or comforting words that he could understand.

Here is where the Internet can help. We've set up a program with the Kosovo Internet centers and other places in Europe that we call "Video Visit." It's simple, and it works like this. My organization, WiRED, buys video-equipped computers for hospitals where the kids are being treated. Before surgery, and at regular intervals during recovery, we get the kids in front of video cameras. Back at the centers in Kosovo and Albania, the parents and siblings gather in front of another video camera connected to a computer. Through the Internet, we join the children and their parents for a "Video Visit." The doctors we're working with in Italy think the contact can even speed the recovery. That remains to be seen, of course, but think what this demonstration of human communication can contribute to the soul of democracy.

An open channel between a mother and her sick child. Doctors downloading new treatments from the West. Reporters checking out the international press. Students swapping information with students half a world away. They offer evidence that the Internet is providing a fair demonstration of how the virtues of a free society can be appealingly communicated to millions of people preparing for their first steps toward democracy.

The Internet Harms Society

by Deborah C. Sawyer

About the author: *Deborah C. Sawyer is president of Information Plus, a research service firm, and the author of* Sawyer's Success Tactics for Information Businesses.

The preponderance of false and misleading information on the Internet, coupled with a declining ability to think critically, spells big trouble ahead.

According to many who predict the future, we will all sit at computers to work, play, shop, socialize, and more. Such futurists describe this scenario in glowing terms, but those of us who work hands-on with information content disagree. The way people request, process, and use information suggests that we are moving in a troubling direction.

What many of the techno gurus overlook, in sketching their design for the future, is human nature. On the cusp of the twenty-first century, eight catalysts of chaos are preparing to lead our society astray. By not paying attention to these catalysts, we are much like the people of the fable who did not pay the Pied Piper, causing him to lead their children away.

More Access, Less Sharing

The first of these catalysts is increased access to information, thanks to the proliferation of sources on the Internet and the World Wide Web. We think we are entitled to all the information there is. This has led to feeding-frenzy conditions and a sometimes voyeuristic approach to information. No one wants to entertain the suggestions that information may be private or that it should be restricted to people who understand it. The merest mention of censorship invariably produces howls of dismay.

We want it all, we want it now—but please don't ask any of us to share our own information! Along with this sense of entitlement to information comes a counterforce, a marked decrease in sharing. Legitimate privacy concerns are only part of this trend: It makes sense to be careful with the release of Social Security numbers or credit-card information, but we no longer feel a sense of obligation or civic duty to participate in the collection of information. Survey participation has declined; people do not wish to be interrupted; they don't want to get involved. Survey researchers react with surprise when a human actually answers the phone—especially one willing to answer questions. Who among us hasn't shuffled by the lady with the clipboard at the mall, averting our eyes, so we won't have to take time for a survey?

This phenomenon produces an unfortunate skew of information since available opinions tend to reflect only the views of those willing to release data—often a vocal minority rather than a cross-section of society. This situation is particularly ironic in societies that value free speech; such provisions, though they are written on paper in constitutions, will not survive if they are not exercised by the majority as rights.

Some will counter that the obvious solution is to pay people for their information while conducting surveys over the Internet. But paying people for information will attract those who, first and foremost, need the money. Government policy and societal decisions should not be shaped solely with information contributed by those who are desperate for cash.

More Bad Information

If these two opposing catalysts are not bad enough, consider the third and fourth: the increase in quantity and decrease in quality of information. More and more information of dubious merit proliferates on the Internet and the World Wide Web. This information is highly repetitious, skewed, and often hopelessly inaccurate, but that seems to escape the notice of those who believe in the virtues of cyberspace. Unlike trade magazines, newspapers, and other "archaic" print sources, the Internet does not vet its information: There is little copy editing or fact checking. Anything and everything gets circulated in electronic form, including wild rumors, junk science, appalling misinformation, and inane gibberish.

An unfortunate by-product of the current cybercraze is that some people believe as gospel truth anything that comes out of a computer. This is particularly noticeable among those in their teens and 20s, who have not learned the necessary skills to seek out alternate sources and verify information.

The proliferation of sources in this so-called Information Age masks another development: the consolidation of reasonably reliable information into the hands of fewer and fewer organizations. This consolidation applies as much to print sources as it does to electronic information. Whenever such consolidation occurs, competition dwindles, leaving a world with declining quality of data. For example, in the 1950s there were often two or three directories or "industry bibles" per industry. Today there is usually only one, and the level of detail is down significantly.

> *"More and more information of dubious merit proliferates on the Internet and the World Wide Web."*

Then there is the impermanence that characterizes all electronic information; if you find information of value on the Internet and don't download it right away, six months later the chances are you will not be able to find it. Imagine the horror stories if the information is needed to prove a point—as in a legal case—and cannot be found!

More Barriers Between People

Contrary to what the gurus predict, technology fosters the fifth catalyst, an increase in barriers, an excuse to dodge person-to-person interaction. Many organizations with a mandate to collect and disseminate information to the public use their Web sites as a way to avoid answering questions person-to-person. Phone up an association or a government department and you are more than likely to be told to consult the Web site. If a human actually answers the phone to tell you this, the phone will then quickly be hung up in your ear. The fact that the Web site may not answer your particular questions seems to be of little concern.

As is obvious to anyone who has ever used it, Web site information is controlled by those putting up the site. The danger here, if we allow this trend to continue, is that we will become not a society that asks the questions it wants to ask or the questions that need to be asked, but one that asks only the questions for which answers already exist. There is already a marked tendency among younger people to conclude that their questions were not

> *"Technology fosters . . . an excuse to dodge person-to-person interaction."*

worth asking in the first place if they could not find answers on a Web site. Even twenty-somethings employed at professional research firms exhibit this tendency. When desired data does not magically appear on the computer screen, they consider their jobs finished and resist the notion of picking up the phone to track the answer down. This is a very dangerous phenomenon.

Discourtesy and Dishonesty

The increase in barriers coincides with a marked decrease in courtesy, the sixth catalyst propelling us in a very different direction than the bright future the techno gurus prophesy. Even with older technologies such as the telephone, it has already become acceptable to not return phone calls or respond to messages. With the newer forms such as e-mail, impatience often produces strongly worded exchanges. Imprecise use of language in electronic commerce leads to "flaming," the electronic equivalent of being chewed-out in public. This is all part of a larger trend of rude behavior. No society anywhere in human history grew to greatness by placing a premium on discourtesy. The general level of rudeness does not bode well for future human connectedness.

Discourtesy goes hand-in-hand with the seventh catalyst, increase in dishonesty. The Information Age is rife with cheating and plagiarism. This produces a climate of deceit. And those who do cheat—downloading essays off the Internet to pass courses, for example—should stop to think: At what point will they themselves be cheated?

Losing Our Skills

Those who use the Internet for deceit, such as plagiarizing essays, tend not to have the know-how to do their own work, and this leads to the greatest catalyst of chaos: the decrease in skills. The ability to access information—and lots of it—does not create an ability to evaluate it. All the catalysts described up to now are really supporting actors to this most central player. Thirty years of experimentation in the schools with reading methodologies, mathematics, and other basics have eroded

"The Information Age is rife with cheating and plagiarism."

these real skills while fostering pseudo-skills such as self-esteem. Young people believe anything on the computer, lack the know-how to verify what they find there, and think that, if the information isn't on the Web, then the questions aren't worth asking in the first place.

The result? Into a world with widespread access to information, controlled by fewer and fewer parties, comes a generation with a naive belief in the computer and few skills to defend itself. The stage is set for this generation to be led astray: Get ready to welcome the electronic Pied Piper.

If this steadily burgeoning chaos is allowed to take its full course, no foreign power intent on conquering a country such as the United States in the early part of the next century would need bother with cumbersome things like aircraft carriers, amphibious vehicles, and ordnance. A much simpler way to take over a country will be to simply post information on the Internet and bamboozle the people.

Those who laugh and say it could not happen need to remember that it already has—almost. On the evening of October 30, 1938, "The War of the Worlds," a radio program that described a fictional invasion of Earth by Martians, was broadcast in America. A substantial number of radio listeners believed what they heard—and ran like rabbits. They took to their cars, they took to the highways, some even committed suicide to escape the dreadful events being broadcast. But not all listeners responded this way. What characterized those who did not panic is that they sought out sources of information other than the radio. Some made visual checks of the street and noticed people going into restaurants and coming out of movies and hailing cabs; the National Guard had not been called out. These people, therefore, reserved judgment. Others consulted Broadcast Week, discovered that they were hearing a scheduled broadcast, and sat down to listen. But those who relied on the information coming out of the radio, and believed in that single source, panicked.

Those who want a technology-drenched future where we spend our lives hooked up to computers may not believe an entire nation could be duped by false information on the Internet. They should consider this more recent anecdote. In a large North American city, a story appeared on the Internet about a woman who was assaulted by her taxi driver late one night. The woman was supposedly a member of the advertising and communications community, and her story attracted attention from other advertising agencies, public relations firms, and the like, spreading like wildfire. People called up their listservs and zapped the story all around the city. It multiplied like mushrooms after the rain. Even when the police investigated and could not find the woman, could not find the taxi driver, and further verified that the cab company in question did not even have a cab with the number given, the hoax did not stop spreading. Even when the truth was known, supposedly reasonable, well-educated people preferred to believe the lie simply because it appeared on the Internet.

It is time for those who anticipate a computer- or infotech-dependent future to recognize the downside of their visions. We must consider where the electronic Pied Piper is leading us.

The Information Age Has Not Dramatically Improved Everyday Life

by Phillip J. Longman

About the author: *Phillip J. Longman is a reporter for* U.S. News & World Report.

America, everyone knows, is in the midst of a high-tech boom. Each week brings news of faster chips, speedier relays, and broader bandwidths. Yet how does today's pace of technological change compare with that of two or three generations ago? Do we really have reason to proclaim that we are living in an age of super-inventiveness?

To gauge how today's technological marvels stack up against earlier ones, just flick on Nick at Nite and watch any of those family sitcoms from the 1950s. When Ozzie and Harriet made their television debut on Oct. 3, 1952, they didn't have Internet access or a cellphone, but their living conditions were otherwise very close to those of today's middle-class families.

They had indoor plumbing, electric lights, a car, television, telephone, refrigerator, blender, vacuum cleaner, and probably an automatic laundry washer and dryer. If a time machine magically transported the Nelsons to a typical middle-class household in 2000, they would find most of the technologies of ordinary life improved in quality but otherwise familiar.

They'd recognize the telephone and need only a second to realize we now use push buttons instead of rotary dials. They'd recognize the television even if, like most everyone else these days, they'd have trouble programming the VCR. They might be startled by the gas mileage obtained by a modern automobile, but they would have no trouble knowing how to drive one. Picking up the morning newspaper, they might be puzzled by references to AIDS and genetically modified food but would understand references to nuclear power, air conditioning, plastics, jet airplanes, rockets, radar, and even computers.

Yet now suppose that a time machine magically transported Ozzie and Harriet half a century in the opposite direction. As viewers of the PBS series The 1900 House can attest, even middle-class existence at that time was extraordinarily arduous. Without the benefit of penicillin, even a small cut could prove fatal. Life expectancy at birth was but 47.3 years, compared with 68.3 years in 1950. Most doctors lacked any scientific training, and the bottles in their bags contained little more than alcohol and opiates. Lack of refrigeration, poor sanitary conditions, and adulteration meant millions died from spoiled or tainted food, while epidemics of scarlet fever, yellow fever, and smallpox offered constant reminders of life's fragility.

> *"Do we really have reason to proclaim that we are living in an age of super-inventiveness?"*

Even affluent households were illuminated with gaslights that were expensive to run and prone to explosion. Without electricity, there were no laundry machines, vacuum cleaners, or other mechanical means to purge the household of dirt and germs. The air stank of coal dust, manure, and rotting garbage thrown from windows. Only the super-rich could afford a car, and the vast majority of families did without indoor plumbing. Further deprived of access to a telephone, and without even a radio to provide entertainment, Ozzie and Harriet would have felt nearly as stifled and out of place in the dark and chilly rooms of The 1900 House as would their great-grandchildren.

The Slowing Pace of Progress

Measuring the rate of technological progress over time is hardly easy, but one statistic strongly suggests why Ozzie and Harriet probably would have found it more disorienting to travel 50 years into the past than 50 years into the future. The number tracks how efficiently the economy uses labor, capital, raw materials, and new technology. Economists call it total-factor productivity. Between 1913 and 1972, it grew by an annual average of 1.08 percent. Then between 1972 and 1995, for reasons economists are still debating, the rate of improvement collapsed to less than one fiftieth that of the previous era, despite a widespread adoption of computers.

In recent years, the rate of productivity growth in America has quickened, but the official statistics are deceiving because they mask the dramatic disparity in how different sectors of the economy are performing. In a much-discussed piece for the *Journal of Economic Perspectives,* Robert J. Gordon, a respected economist from Northwestern University, performs a careful analysis of U.S. productivity trends since 1995, adjusting for changes in the business cycle, quality of the labor supply, and other technical factors. He finds, predictably enough, that we have become very efficient at making computers and, to a lesser extent, other durable manufactured items. But such production accounts for only 12 percent of the U.S. economy, Gordon notes. For the other 88 percent, comprising banks, stores, and other service providers, rates of productivity growth have actually been falling slightly.

There's another way to grasp how comparatively undramatic today's high technology has been in its effect on ordinary life. Think of the life experience of a relative who was born near the beginning of the 20th century. My grandfather, who came into this world in 1905, used to tell me about how, when he was a boy growing up in Cincinnati, his schoolmates would rush to the window and gawk if an automobile happened by. Lester Longman, who was born 20 months after the Wright brothers' first flight, lived to see not only men walk on the moon but the explosion of the space shuttle *Challenger,* too.

Yet where is the invention today that makes schoolchildren rush to the windows? I was 13 years old at the time of the first moon shot and, like many kids my age, wondered if the adults were right that my generation one day would build suburbs up there. But it's now been 28 years since any human being has even left Earth's orbit. Meanwhile, there has been virtually no advance in jet propulsion systems save to make them quieter and more fuel efficient, and air travel times have actually lengthened. Until the cancellation of the Concorde flights in July [2000], following the fiery crash in Paris, it was possible to cross the Atlantic at speeds of up to 1,350 mph. Now the fastest available flight goes less than half that speed. Even if the Concorde is eventually returned to service, the 31-year-old plane is so antique that its useful life is limited, and there is nothing on the planning boards to replace it.

> *"There is a distinction to be made between inventions that are merely sophisticated . . . and those that fundamentally alter the human condition."*

Similarly, though automobiles now contain microchips and some can talk to you, in most parts of the country it actually takes longer to drive from point A to point B than it did 30 years ago, because of worsening congestion. Over the past 15 years, while the population of major urban areas rose by 22 percent, time spent in traffic jams soared by 235 percent. In 1938, the 20th Century Limited, pulled by a steam engine, sped from New York to Chicago in 16 hours. Today, Amtrak's version of the train, drawn by a high-tech, fuel-injected diesel with computer diagnostics on board, takes five hours longer. . . .

Information Technology Has Not Altered the Human Condition

There is a distinction to be made between inventions that are merely sophisticated—such as, say, personal digital assistants—and those that fundamentally alter the human condition. The invention of the light bulb created more useful hours in each day for virtually every human being. The electric motor directly raised the productivity in every sphere of life, from speeding up assembly lines to creating so many labor-saving devices in the home that millions of housewives were able to join the paid work force. The internal combustion engine allowed for mass, high-speed transportation of both people and freight while also opening up vast regions of cheap land to suburban development. The materials revolution that brought us petroleum refining, synthetic chemicals, and pharmaceuticals involved learning to rearrange molecules in ways that made raw materials fundamentally more valuable. Without the genetically improved seeds that brought us the "Green Revolution" of the late 1960s and '70s, there would be mass starvation.

Can we make any parallel claim about the single greatest technology of our own time? It remains possible that networked computers and other new information technologies will one day create similar, societywide bursts in productivity, health, and wealth. Yet to date, the marginal gains computers have brought to communications are modest even compared with the improvements made by the telegraph. The first trans-Atlantic telegraph cable in 1866 reduced the time required to send a message from New York to London from about a week to a few minutes. Notes economist Alan Blinder: "No modern IT innovation has, or I dare say will, come close to such a gain!"

And with computers, it is also possible that their largest benefits have already been realized. Consider the gain in productivity achieved when offices started converting from typewriters to word processors. A circa-1978 Wang 10A word processor with daisy-wheel printer, though expensive and difficult to operate, offered a quantum leap over the typewriter because it allowed users to correct and edit documents and manage mailing lists at far greater speed. Every year since, word processors have become cheaper, more powerful, and easier to use, but the marginal gain in productivity thereby achieved continues to decline. Indeed, for many users, converting to, say, the latest generation of Word, after having already invested in learning to use WordPerfect five years before, entails a net loss of productivity.

Linking computers to the Internet might seem to offer large gains in productivity, but as Professor Gordon points out, the evidence from the marketplace suggests the opposite. Even with Internet access now easily available, sales of computers are now no higher than one would expect

> *"The marginal gains computers have brought to communications are modest even compared with the improvements made by the telegraph."*

given their continually falling price. The implication, notes Gordon, is that the incremental benefit of additional computer power continues to shrink.

But what if, as is widely promised, the Internet soon offers consumers the ability to download videos at a low price, or to conduct videoconferences, or shop for the best values with no more effort than using a television remote? As Gordon and other economists point out, the returns to the economy as a whole would be much smaller than might be imagined. This is because the growth of E-commerce largely involves simply substituting existing forms of economic activity—such as visiting a bookstore, renting a video, or calling a travel agent—with a virtual equivalent. Yes, there may be a potential gain in efficiency to be had from buying a book online, but it comes at the cost of cannibalizing existing bookstore sales. By contrast, internal combustion engines and electric motors, while displacing steam technology, also made possible wholly new products, ranging from aircraft to air conditioners, for which there was little or no previously existing substitute.

One technological feature of our times Ozzie and Harriet would find extraordinary is the gadgets we throw out. In 1954, it took the average worker 562 hours of labor to earn enough to buy a color TV. The machine was so expensive that only a few families owned one, and if it broke, as it frequently did, you got it repaired. By 1997, the average worker earned enough in just 23 hours to purchase a 25-inch-screen color TV, and if it broke, as it infrequently did, it most likely went in the trash. The Bureau of Labor Statistics predicts that the ranks of "electronic home entertainment equipment repairers" will continue to decline by at least 1 percent a year through 2008, owing to decreased demand.

Greater Efficiency

In the history of technology, what most distinguishes the present age is not the creation of great new inventions but our genius for re-engineering and manufacturing previously existing machines and gadgets with ever greater efficiency, so that their price declines even as their quality improves. According to calculations by the Federal Reserve Bank of Dallas, the average worker in 1997 could earn enough to buy a new Ford Taurus in just 1,365 hours, whereas his counter-part in 1955 needed to work 1,638 hours to afford the celebrated but much inferior Ford Fairlane. Stoves, dishwashers, refrigerators, washers and dryers, window air conditioners, and most other accouterments of modern middle-class life have fallen in real price even more dramatically since the 1950s. Even homes themselves are cheaper, with the price per square foot dropping from 6.5 times the average worker's hourly wage in 1956 to 5.6 times in 1996.

In their time, Ozzie and Harriet lived much better than the average American family; now their standard of living would be average, or even below average if one accounts for the improved quality and lower price of the familiar electrical devices and appliances that filled their home. That the mass of American families now has access to television at all, let alone one in every bedroom, is in itself an amazing achievement, as is the ability of the global economy to provide millions of American teenagers with their own cars, computers, and stereos. But this democratization of access to existing technology, while it has obvious and mostly salutary social implications, is hardly the mark of a great age of invention. Perhaps another Thomas Edison is hard at work, using nanotechnology or bioengineering to invent new machines that are truly revolutionary and transforming. But he or she has not succeeded yet.

Online Communities Cannot Substitute for Real-Life Communities

by Dinesh D'Souza

About the author: *Dinesh D'Souza is a research scholar at the American Enterprise Institute and the author of* The Virtue of Prosperity: Finding Values in an Age of Techno-Affluence.

There has been an undeniable erosion of community attachments in the United States in the past few decades. Champions of technology—a group I call the techno-utopians—believe the Internet can reverse that decline through "electronic neighborhoods," where people form the same kinds of social bonds they once formed in physical neighborhoods.

Can technology help to restore community? I believe it can, but not for the reason given by the techno-utopians.

Cybercommunity is a concept that has caught on in the tech world. Jeff Bezos, founder and CEO of Amazon.com, defines a community as "neighbors helping neighbors," and contends that companies like Amazon.com foster community by allowing people to swap ideas and product reviews online. Steve Case, the CEO of America Online, argues that AOL is more than a money-making enterprise; it is a catalyst for the restoration of community.

These claims are met with understandable skepticism. In a recent book, Stephen Doheny-Farina writes, "The society of the Net isolates individuals. Once we begin to divorce ourselves from geographic space and start investing ourselves in virtual geographies, we further the dissolution of our physical communities."

Mr. Doheny-Farina's premise is that authentic community requires a physical sense of place, and of belonging. How can you call 1,000 people sitting alone in their computer rooms typing away a community?

Virtual Gathering Places

Who is right? To find out, I've been visiting various Web sites and online gathering places that promise "relationships" and "community," and I must confess these concepts take on a strange new meaning on the Web. First, there are commercial sites like Amazon and eBay, where people exchange information about their purchases. The Net undeniably has made markets more efficient, but it's hard to describe these capitalist transactions as constituting community.

Then I visited "multiuser dungeons" and online games such as "Ultima Online," where thousands of players take on virtual identities, live in virtual homes, hold virtual jobs, and even marry and have virtual families, all while performing feats like killing dragons and one another.

> *"How can you call 1,000 people sitting alone in their computer rooms typing away a community?"*

Many people find these games addictive, spending hours a day living out a virtual existence as a dragon slayer or a captain on an interplanetary voyage.

Even so, this is not community. The reason is given by sociologist Robert Nisbet, who writes that community is a set of relationships characterized by personal intimacy, emotional depth, moral commitment, social cohesion, and continuity in time. This is a demanding list of criteria, but Professor Nisbet seems right in pointing out that traditional communities absorb the whole person, not just a particular role or interest.

The Web fosters voluntary associations among people who have a specialized interest. People who study Persian poetry or play chess, people in wheelchairs, and people who listen to Jim Croce, can through the Web find others who share their passions. Techno-utopian Virginia Postrel argues that in this respect, cybercommunities are better than real communities because they allow us to choose our affiliations.

But the argument for chosen affiliations cuts both ways. "Voluntary associations" tend to restrict our associations to those who are most like us.

C.S. Lewis once said one of the great benefits of involuntary communities—including the family—is that they enable us to discover the virtues of people whom we might never have chosen to hang out with.

Mr. Lewis's point is repeatedly confirmed through experience: The annoying fellow who happens to be your neighbor or your brother turns out to be very loyal or deep-thinking or empathetic in relating to old people. A life primarily shaped by voluntary associations is one that cuts itself off from the broader range of human experiences.

So, my conclusion is that, while the relationships we develop on the Web may be useful or entertaining, they are generally too thin and ephemeral to constitute genuine community. The Web can supplement physical community but it cannot replace it.

But while real community can't be sustained through the Web, this technology has created a paradoxical effect. Because more of us can work out of our homes, we can choose our ideal communities and spend more time in them.

Until a year ago, my family lived in Washington, D.C. We had to live there because I am a research scholar at a research institute based in the nation's capital. Washington is an exciting place to be if you care about politics, but it is a transient place, perfect for single people. I didn't feel it was a healthy place to raise a family. But for years, there was no reasonable prospect of moving because of my work.

Now, because of the research capacity of the Web, and because of other communications technologies like faxes and e-mail, I can live anywhere. Recently, our family moved to a more family-oriented neighborhood in San Diego. Our new setting is closer to nature, and more conducive to forming social and civic bonds.

Physicist Freeman Dyson writes that "the typical English village today is not primarily engaged in farming." Hidden inside the homes with thatched roofs are high-tech firms. The residents have rebuilt the dilapidated church, Dyson says, and the church bells ring again. Here, I believe, is a model that will eventually be replicated widely in the West.

The old economy pulled us away from the village and toward the city, where the jobs were, but now we are seeing a reversal of the pattern. Slowly but surely, technology is making the lasting connections afforded by the village viable again.

The Information Age May Not Foster Democracy

by Andrew L. Shapiro

About the author: *Andrew L. Shapiro is a journalist, lawyer, and author of* The Control Revolution: How the Internet Is Putting Individuals in Charge and Changing the World We Know.

The Internet is inherently democratizing.

Wrong. Pundits and politicians alike are fond of making this claim, but it is an empty truism and a dangerous one at that. The Internet does have strong democratic proclivities. As a vast forum that encourages "many-to-many" interaction, the Net makes it possible for citizens around the world to participate in public dialogue. Its decentralized structure helps individuals bypass gate-keepers and control the flow of information and goods. And its nonproprietary nature—no one owns the technical protocols that make the Net work—suggests a degree of openness and public purpose. Yet these features are shaped by malleable computer code and subject to alteration, often in ways that may not be obvious to nontechies. Saudi Arabia, for example, did not give its citizens online access until it had effectively tinkered with the code of the Net to filter out all "objectionable" material. And Iran programmed the chat rooms of its closed online network so that only two people could speak to one another at a time. (Apparently, allowing three people to caucus openly was too threatening.)

Technology design, in short, will be at the heart of various power struggles in the digital age. We should not be surprised to see governments and corporations trying to shape the code of the Net to preserve their authority or profitability. But code is not everything. Even if we could lock in the democratic features of the Internet, the ultimate political impact of this technology (or any other) must be judged on more than design. We must also consider the way a technology is used and the social environment in which it is deployed. Taking all three of these factors into account—design, use, and environment—it should be clear that the Internet may suppress as well as promote democracy.

The Information Revolution Has Not Put an End to Censorship

Freedom of speech will flourish in the digital age.

Maybe. The Net empowers individual speakers, allowing them to spread their views far and wide with tens of thousands of e-mail newsletters, new formats for music storage online, even 24-hour personal Web-cam sites. The political benefits are clear. In 1996, for example, Serbian prodemocracy activists used the Internet to "broadcast" radio programming from Radio B92, a protest station that had been forcefully shut down by President Slobodan Milosevic. Within days of their cybercast, the broadcasts had been heard around the world and international pressure caused Milosevic to reopen the station.

Those who use cutting-edge technology to speak to the world, however, may incur resistance. When Milosevic shut down Radio B92 at the beginning of NATO's 1999 bombing campaign, the station once again re-routed its programming to the Net. But this time, an embattled Milosevic ignored global requests to let the station broadcast freely and placed B92 under puppet management. In China, Lin Hai, a software entrepreneur, received a two-year sentence in January for supplying e-mail addresses to dissidents abroad who published a prodemocracy Web magazine. And in Burma, where all interactive technology is tightly regulated, a supporter of the prodemocracy movement died in prison, where he was being held for using a fax machine without a license.

Those governments were practicing censorship the old-fashioned way: with force. But even without government interference, a new information landscape may emerge that is differ-

"The Internet may suppress as well as promote democracy."

ent from the democratic free-speech tradition we know. The vaunted "marketplace of ideas" presumes a public forum in which an idea can be aired and judged based on its veracity, not the resources behind it. Of course, there have always been different levels of access to this marketplace depending on a speaker's status and wealth (it helps, for example, when you can afford to buy advertisements to spread your message). But the proliferation of information—and, correspondingly, the proliferation of filtering technology—presents the possibility of a much more cutthroat market for speech. And that will likely mean paying to be heard. In a world where attention is increasingly scarce, the voices of many of the Internet's early beneficiaries—individuals, nonprofits, and small businesses—may, like the voices of those on ham radio or public-access cable channels, become lost in cyberspace, drowned out by the din of speech that is paid for by the highest bidder.

Clamping Down on the Exchange of Ideas

Governments cannot effectively regulate cyberspace.

Think again. For years, creative cyber-rights advocates have tried to elude draconian state regulation of the Internet by pushing the idea that online interactions occur on some distant frontier beyond the reach of "meatspace" governments. Not only is state regulation of cyberspace illegitimate, they say, it simply cannot be done. As a defense against censorship, it is a clever argument. But for the most part, it is just not true.

In addition to wielding an iron hand, authoritarian nations are increasingly adopting a more sly silicon touch in order to control what their citizens can read and hear online. Filtering software and protocols such as the Platform for Internet Content Selection (which, like bar codes on commercial packaging, standardize labels on Internet content) may make censorship easier than in the predigital era. Instead of confiscating underground books or pamphlets, governments can simply route all Internet communication through electronic gateways known as proxy servers. These powerful computers act as high-tech sieves, sifting out whatever is deemed subversive or offensive. China uses proxy servers to exclude a good deal of foreign content—from dissident sites to, on occasion, the *New York Times* and CNN. And Singapore requires Internet service providers to use filtering technology to block certain pornographic sites. Of course, there may be ways to evade such machinations, but authoritarian regimes faced with the unfettered flow of digital speech are unlikely to yield easily.

> *"Authoritarian nations are increasingly adopting a more sly silicon touch in order to control what their citizens can read and hear online."*

Even liberal Western nations have put blunt Internet regulations in place and pursued logic-defying prosecutions. In 1997, for example, the German state of Bavaria prosecuted Felix Somm, the local head of the online service Compuserve, because a Compuserve subscriber used the service to obtain illegal pornographic materials. Compuserve did not produce the materials and neither Somm nor any other company representative had reason to know how that one subscriber was using the service. Nevertheless, Somm himself was found guilty of trafficking in pornography. The United States has been particularly aggressive in controlling the development and export of encryption. The U.S. government has flexed its regulatory muscle in a variety of ways, imposing trade restrictions, pushing legislation, and pressuring industry to embrace the Clipper Chip, a weak encryption standard. Until late in 1996, the Clinton administration actually classified strong encryption as a munition, making it a crime to send or carry it out of the country (export is still forbidden, only now the Department of Commerce is in charge). Washington has also tried, with less success, to regulate sexual materials online. In 1997, the Supreme Court struck down the Communications Decency Act, a speech restriction so vague that a person who published common obscenities on the Web could have been imprisoned. Undeterred, Congress went back to the drawing board and enacted the Child Online Protection Act, a more subtle attempt to curb cybersmut that has nonetheless been enjoined by a federal court.

From content control and privacy to intellectual property, electronic commerce, and the Y2K problem, legislators at the state, national, and international levels are becoming intricately involved in setting digital policy. With more than 200 Internet-related bills considered during the 105th U.S. Congress alone, the idea that government cannot control the Internet has become pretty laughable. Of course, not all regulation is bad regulation. The European Union has implemented a directive on information privacy that sets strict limits on the collection and use of personal data (limits that have left U.S. privacy protection looking threadbare by comparison and nearly launched a transatlantic trade war, as the directive limits information transfer to noncompliant countries such as the United States). The real question, therefore, is whether lawmakers will regulate wisely and deftly or anxiously and incompetently. . . .

Information Has a Price

Information wants to be free.

It does? This popular cybermaxim derives from a claim by Internet guru Stewart Brand in his 1987 book, *The Media Lab:* "Information wants to be free because it has become so cheap to distribute, copy and recombine. . . . It wants to be expensive because it can be immeasurably valuable to the recipient." There is a degree of truth to both of Brand's statements. Observers of all stripes have noted that copyright law will no longer work because the Internet and other digital tools bear a striking resemblance to a giant copying machine, allowing software, video, music, and text to be pirated with the push of a button. Yet, at the same time, as information becomes the coin of the global realm, powerful actors are devising ever more ingenious ways to lock it up and charge for it.

Most notably, the entertainment, publishing, and software industries—with the help of allies in legislatures and international bodies such as the World Intellectual Property Organization—have been developing new ways to protect their intangible assets. These "copyright maximalists," as law professor Pamela Samuelson calls them, have pushed for unprecedented statutory protection for databases (collections of facts not protected by copyright law, which covers only original expression). And they have worked to create technological protection measures that could, again, be more favorable to owners than traditional intellectual-property statutes. These innovations include the ubiquitous clickwrap contracts that are found online—fine-print agreements "signed" by clicking an Okay button—as well as "trusted systems" technology, which regulates how digital information is used: how many times it can be viewed, whether it can be duplicated, and so on. In a sense, it is intellectual-property protection without the need for cops and courts.

What is missing from these efforts—and from Brand's aphorism—is the notion that information needs to be protected in the public interest. Copyright law, after all, is not just about safeguarding the property of authors (or, more realistically, megapublishers). It is about striking a delicate constitutional balance between providing incentives for creativity and making valuable works available to the public. Innovations such as database protection, clickwrap contracts, and trusted systems could, if not carefully limited by legislatures and courts, tip the balance too far toward information owners. The public domain would shrivel up, to society's disadvantage. The international legal community must figure out how to apply the principles of balance that underlie existing intellectual-property laws to the digital world. . . .

International Relations Remains a Tricky Business

The Internet is redefining international diplomacy.

Perhaps. Although the Net is not inherently democratizing, in some instances it does seem to be causing political and social hierarchies to unravel, gradually transferring power from massive, entrenched institutions down toward the level of nonprofits, communities, and even individuals. As a result, fields such as international relations may become more egalitarian, as small nongovernmental organizations find themselves on more equal footing with states and multinational corporations. Human rights groups, for example, may find that they can use the Net to garner attention instantly and internationally, embarrassing rights abusers into ceasing brutal practices. At the same time, relief organizations may be able to harness the speed and depth of the Net to increase the efficiency and impact of their efforts. In the near future, however, international politics will still largely take place within the existing frameworks of negotiation and decision making. And again, much will depend on whether powerful actors resist the democratic potential of the Net by trying to regulate its code. Encryption, for example, the technology that allows communications to be scrambled and kept private, is a vital tool of human rights work; it allows field workers to collect, transmit, and store communications in a way that does not compromise the safety of victims and witnesses. If governments outlaw or restrict strong encryption, human rights workers—and their clients—will be deprived of an important digital asset, one that would help them to take on corrupt powers.

> *"As national boundaries become increasingly permeable . . . individuals will have less incentive even to identify themselves as citizens of a certain country."*

The Internet will enhance cross-cultural understanding and empathy.

Not necessarily. Four decades ago, social scientist Daniel Lerner argued that the introduction of mass media into developing countries allows for a broadening of empathy. Radio, television, and newspapers, in other words, can educate citizens and encourage them to care about the plight of fellow community members. For all their other failings, mass media can help to cultivate a sense of common identity and unity across broad distances.

Similarly, if we were to use the Net to open ourselves up to new social and cultural experiences, we could do wonders for cooperation and mutual understanding at the local, national, and international levels. But the ability the Net gives us to endlessly filter and personalize information means that, more than ever before, we can also build virtual gated communities where we never have to interact with people who are different from ourselves. Will people actually be inclined to narrow their horizons this way? One would hope not. Unfortunately, theories of social psychology such as selective avoidance suggest that many people may be inclined to use their new power over information to reinforce existing political beliefs rather than to challenge themselves. We could lose our "agora in the media," as communications scholar Ithiel de Sola Pool called it.

If this happens, communal conversations could be cut up into an endless number of isolated exchanges. Local activists would have difficulty competing with virtual communities for the attention of their neighbors. Nations might have difficulty resolving complex issues such as abortion or immigration when citizens can opt out of a shared base of information so easily. And citizens might feel less of a connection with, and less of an obligation toward, one another. Indeed, as national boundaries become increasingly permeable and irrelevant to networked life, individuals will have less incentive even to identify themselves as citizens of a certain country. Without a sense of national community, individuals may increasingly vote according to narrow self-interest rather than support policies that protect the common good.

Even as the global nature of the Net promises to let us shrink the world, compromise between different nations and peoples may be more difficult if we replace fading national borders with new ones based on prejudice or self-indulgent preference. "In the worst case scenario," as political commentator E.J. Dionne puts it, "the global village becomes a global Bosnia. . . ."

Much of the World Has Not Benefited from the Information Age

by Fabian A. Koss

About the author: *Fabian A. Koss is the youth liaison in the special programs section of the Office of External Relations of the Inter-American Development Bank, an institution that works to accelerate economic and social development in Latin America and the Caribbean.*

For the first time in history, half the world's population is under the age of 20. Nearly one billion children have been born in the 1990s alone. As of June 2000, population experts estimate that nearly 523 million people are living in Latin America and the Caribbean, and 269 million of them are under 24 years of age. Of the regions' total population, children make up 51 percent—one out of every two people in the region is a child or a youth aged 24 and under. In countries including Bolivia, Guatemala, Haiti and Nicaragua, children and youth make up 60 percent or more of the population. The vast majority of these children and youth will grow up during a time of social, economic, technological and political changes that will affect them profoundly. Such changes and the growth in the number of children will have far-reaching implications for governments, economies, communities and the environment. The future of the world has never been so heavily dependent on a single generation.

As we advance into the 21st century, extraordinary advances have been made to improve the lives of children. There has been more progress in the 20th century related to the health and well-being of children than there was in all the previous centuries combined. Deadly childhood diseases like polio have been virtually wiped out. Almost every indicator of health, wealth, safety, nutrition, environmental quality and social conditions indicates rapid improvement over the past century. Among the most significant trends are increased life expectancy, falling infant mortality rates, and a large decrease in the incidence of major killer diseases including tuberculosis, typhoid and pneumonia.

Yet despite powerful progress, challenges persist and new ones emerge as we enter the 21st century—both in the developing and developed worlds. At the dawn of the new millennium, the United Nations Development Program (UNDP) found that worldwide, 100 million children are still living or working on the streets. Infant mortality remains a serious problem: 8 percent of infants do not live to see their fifth birthday. Each day, 30,000 children die from communicable diseases. And 2.8 billion of the world's 6 billion people live on less than $2 per day—1.2 billion live on less than $1 per day. Economic, geographic and social barriers limit millions of youth from developing their individual potential. As a result, increased numbers of youth are living on the streets, vulnerable to crime and drugs and without hope for a healthy future.

The Promise of Technology

While childhood poverty, sickness and despair may still frequently prevail, technological advancement can provide new opportunities for children in education and employment. A technologically savvy youth is important not only in terms of education, but also in terms of playing an important role in employment and in a country's development. The bridging of the digital divide is critical to the circumvention of the multifarious problems afflicting children around the world. Educators across the United States spent nearly $6 billion in 2000 building a technologically equipped educational system. And the numbers show the results. In the US, there is slightly more than one computer for every five students. The ratio of students to an internet-connected computer is almost as good, about eight to one. Notwithstanding such technologically advanced schools, there is still much to do. Teachers in the US, for example, must be trained to make better use of technology in the classroom. Yet computer access and use in US classrooms is incredibly advanced when compared to the developing world. In most countries, the problem begins with just being able to obtain computers.

> *"The bridging of the digital divide is critical to the circumvention of the multifarious problems afflicting children around the world."*

Without an educated body of youth prepared to meet the global labor force's needs, a country is relegated to painfully slow progress as more productive and well-paying jobs are sent elsewhere. The International Labor Organization (ILO) estimates that over the next 10 years, despite a slowing in the growth rate of the global labor force, there will still be about 460 million new, young jobseekers, most of them in developing regions, and two-thirds of whom will be in Asia alone. The challenge to employ the record number of youths will be daunting, especially for developing countries. To meet this challenge, countries will need to implement a balanced economic growth strategy. Information and communications technologies (ICTs) are an important engine driving this growth. Holding significant promise in enhancing productivity and creating jobs, ICTs offer prospects for industrialized and developing countries alike to participate in a new global market. Information and communications technologies are tools that can be used to contribute to human development in areas such as education and training and for the delivery of health

> *"The gap between rich and poor countries worsens as the technological divide widens."*

and social services. Through intermediaries, these technologies are able to impact the lives of those for whom direct access is not possible because of poverty, geographical isolation, and literacy and cultural barriers, thereby empowering them and improving their quality of life.

Developed countries first recognized the capacity for wealth creation and subsequently introduced technology jobs that required skilled workers, thereby creating digital opportunities. Companies in turn addressed their technological weaknesses by training their employees to facilitate the transition to more advanced systems. The necessary ingredients to making digital opportunity a reality included political will as well as an information technology infrastructure. The seemingly successful introduction of information technology into the daily lives of so many citizens of the developed world demonstrates that public and private resources are critical to the growth of digital opportunities. Developing countries, on the other hand, will face a difficult future without similar investments. The gap between rich and poor countries worsens as the technological divide widens. Without political support, even significant investments in information technology will result in an ongoing digital divide.

Information Technology + Political Will = Digital Opportunity

Information Technology - Political Will = Digital Divide

The most devastating consequences of the digital divide are the long-term effects it will have on today's youth. Lacking access to technology and computer skills, an entire generation will be disempowered from realizing its full potential to contribute to society. Countries need to recognize their potential, and prepare their youth to be participants in—not waste products of—the technological revolution. These youth represent an opportunity, which if forsaken will only contribute to increased disadvantage.

Identifying the Digital Divide

As used in this [viewpoint], the term "digital divide" refers to the gap between individuals, households, businesses and geographic areas at different socio-economic levels and their opportunities to access information and communication technologies. The digital divide among households appears to depend primarily on two variables: income and education. Other variables, such as household size and type, age, gender, racial and linguistic backgrounds and location also play important roles. The differences in computer and Internet access are large, and they are increasing, but access in lower income groups is rising. Largely through the income effect, the likelihood of an individual's access to information technologies rises as the level of education increases.

Expansion of the digital divide has been exacerbated by the rapid development of technology. The adoption of the Internet as a mass media—defined as time required to reach an audience of 50 million—was the fastest in history. Whereas the radio did not reach mass media status for 38 years, and television required 13 years, the Internet soared from obscurity to 50 million users in just four years. By 1998 there were an estimated 143 million Internet users, with numbers expected to exceed 700 million by [2001]. Some 88 percent of all users in 1998 lived in industrial countries, home to less than 15 percent of the world's people. The US has more computers than the rest of the world combined, and over 100 million Internet users.

At an international level, the most basic and important indicator of the digital divide is the number of access lines per 100 inhabitants. This is the leading indicator for the level of universal service in telecommunications and a fundamental measure of the international digital divide. In 1998, the world's access lines numbered just over 851 million, with some 64.5 percent in OECD [Organisation for Economic Co-operation and Development] countries. In countries with the lowest GDP [gross domestic product] per capita, there were only 1.6 lines per 100 inhabitants in 1998. The two countries with the world's most connected population, Finland and Norway, each have 70 servers per 1,000 inhabitants, the result of investments in high tech infrastructure and education, and general affluence. The Scandinavian countries as a whole realized the importance of information technology early on and quickly worked to get their citizens and corporations connected.

> *"The US has more computers than the rest of the world combined."*

The digital divide is exacerbated by the differential in development pace among developing countries—while most regions saw penetration rates rise during the 1990s, Africa's growth was negligible. Thus, the digital divide is becoming more stratified, with nations like China forming a second tier between the most and least developed countries.

"Digital Apartheid"

Information and communication technology has changed the way we live, the way we work, and the way we approach the day. However, because we are still in the midst of an information revolution, it is extremely difficult to grasp the size and speed of these changes. States that succeed in harnessing these changes can look forward to increased productivity, expanded economic growth, and improved human welfare. Those that do not succeed can look forward to an increased chasm in the ability to compete and accumulate wealth, and a further widening of the economic gap in general. At the beginning of the new millennium, developing nations have an unprecedented opportunity to meet their vital development goals—among them poverty reduction, and basic healthcare and education—more effectively than before. The issues of the digital divide are certainly not all technological.

"The digital have-nots . . . will not be able to become the skilled workers . . . needed to sustain the growth of the Internet economy."

The digital divide first came to public and government attention in 2000 during the G8 summit [a meeting of the Group of Eight industrialized nations: Canada, France, Germany, Great Britain, Italy, Japan, Russia, and the United States] in Okinawa, Japan. At the summit, the Digital Opportunity Taskforce (DOT Force) was conceptualized. The 43-member taskforce includes representatives from governments, the private sector and non-governmental organizations (NGOs). Since its inception, the DOT Force has produced a report that acknowledges that at least one-third of the world's population has yet to make a telephone call, much less use or see a computer. But the report also states that the development goals of the UN—including a greater emphasis on education and gender equality and a reduction in infant mortality rates—can be accomplished more quickly with the aid of the Internet.

When now US Secretary of State General Colin Powell addressed the digital divide issue in *Businessweek* in December 2000, he used an even stronger term: "digital apartheid." He commented: "If digital apartheid persists, we all lose. The digital have-nots will be poorer, more resentful of progress than ever and will not be able to become the skilled workers or potential customers that are needed to sustain the growth of the Internet economy."

Secretary of State Powell was commenting on the enormous power of advanced technology to improve life and make it more prosperous, just and humane. He also implicitly recognized that those who are part of this revolution must be aware of their responsibilities. The use of new technology can reduce the distance between the rich and the poor, but along with the potential benefits of the Internet comes a host of new problems that need to be addressed. Bridging the digital divide does not mean giving everyone a computer with Internet access.

Development specialists and technology executives, Microsoft chairman Bill Gates among them, have questioned the wisdom of wiring developing nations at the expense of immunizing, educating and helping feed the 1.2 billion people in the world who make less than $365 a year. Nevertheless development experts, as well as a chorus of political leaders, argue that devoting more resources to setting up Internet connections in poor areas will, in the long run, provide people with a sense of self-sufficiency.

Chapter 1

Tackling the Digital Divide

The real divide among individuals, organizations and nations is defined by the freedom, incentives and capacity to innovate, and by the opportunity to experiment and take risks. Leaders and governments need to take advantage of the great potential offered by new technologies in a socially responsible way. The digital divide becomes a digital opportunity when public, private and civil society organizations work together to create conditions that enhance the capacity of citizens to use technology. These citizens would then have the chance to become more productive and improve the quality of their lives without jeopardizing this possibility for future generations.

But before governments and organizations around the globe can attempt to tackle the growing chasm between technological haves and have-nots, they first have to define the problem. On 22 July 2000, the White House called on the American private sector during G8 Summit preparations to assist in bridging the global digital divide. Representatives from the international business community, philanthropic foundations and non-governmental organizations presented the White House with a framework. The primary principle of this framework was that sustainable success depends on the active participation of all

> *"Developing nations need comprehensive and strategic approaches to creating national information structures."*

"stakeholders." Private sector leaders have been a key force in the fast adaptation of Internet services in the United States and other developed countries. In order to make the Internet truly global, however, a new set of challenges must be addressed. A specific measurable commitment from governments, multilateral lending institutions, non-governmental organizations and the private sector will be required.

The government of Japan, which hosted the G8 Summit in 2000, invited the World Economic Forum to provide a statement of its members' views on the subject of the global digital divide. In response, the World Economic Forum created the Global Digital Divide Task Force, comprised of leaders in the information technology, communications and entertainment sectors. During Spring 2000, the task force convened in Geneva, Rio de Janeiro and Washington, DC. Such meetings culminated in a statement of proposed policy actions and initiatives necessary to transform the digital divide into an opportunity. The statement also contributed to the creation of the abovementioned DOT Force. Chief among the recommendations were the following:

1. The G8 should take a leadership role by advancing, together with developing countries, a positive vision of the global digital opportunity and by organizing a coordinated effort, backed by high level support from within the international community (and organizations like the UN and World Bank), to assist developing countries in its realization.

2. While much can be achieved through individual efforts, in many cases it
will also be helpful to coordinate the digital programs of multilateral institutions, the international business community, and civil society and philanthropic organizations.

Although the G8 DOT Force represents a commitment from the globe's
most powerful countries, before its recommendations can be formulated and
delivered, governments must act to promote policies to increase competition
in the technology sector. The G8 alone cannot bring about the development of
the poorest countries. This task will require comprehensive action on many
fronts. It is not only about raising money. Success will require the security
and confidence that can only be produced by transparent, strong governance.
The DOT Force must fully take advantage of its resilient partnership with the
UNDP. The UNDP has already deployed Internet nodes in more than 40
countries and trained more than 25,000 organizations and institutions.
Tremendous resources—both financial and in-kind—will be needed to create a
more level playing field.

The framework states that each country must tailor its own solutions, cus-
tomizing a global medium to serve local community needs. In addition to helping developing countries break down barriers to economic and intellectual exchange, the Internet can also assist in preserving a country's cultural heritage.
Yet none of this is possible without critical infrastructure. The best Internet
content cannot reach the citizens of developing countries without communications platforms and devices that are capable of providing access to the online
medium at reasonable costs.

Creating Digital Opportunities

Developing countries must and can seize the digital opportunities, as Costa
Rica, Chile, Peru and South Africa have already demonstrated. But the challenges are tremendous. Only in recent years have multilateral organizations begun to focus on information technology (IT) for development. Developing nations need comprehensive and strategic approaches to creating national
information structures. Decision-makers at each level of government need the
sufficient knowledge to formulate action plans and policies. Effective regulatory bodies need to be created to implement IT policies. In South Africa, the
government has established a governmental regulatory body that oversees the
implementation of ICT-related policies in South Africa.

Canada stands out as an example of a country that has transformed challenge
into opportunity. The Canadian government has made a tremendous commitment to making the country the most connected in the world. Canada On-line
provides all Canadians, including those in rural and remote communities, with
access to Canada's world-leading Information Highway infrastructure.
Canada's Smart Communities is an integrated approach to helping entire communities go on-line to connect local governments, schools, businesses, citizens,

and health and social services. Canada is also combating the global digital divide. NetCorps Canada International offers volunteer internships in developing countries to young leaders with skills in information and communication technologies. These six-month internships are implemented by some of Canada's largest volunteer organizations, including Canada World Youth and the Canadian Society for International Health. This program is financed under the Government of Canada's Youth Employment Strategy.

This incredibly successful initiative is working in part because of the close partnership of the private and public sector businesses. Yet, this very example exhibits the challenge faced by countries of the developing world to create solutions tailored to their own resources.

But alone these ingredients are still not enough. The local population must understand the importance of embracing the tools of the network economy. These tools should be made available, in part, through traditional educational institutions. Another option is to utilize community centers or other centralized public access points to facilitate access while avoiding the need for large infra structure development. . . .

A Choice: Bridge or Widen the Divide

In order to promote sustainable economic and social development, there must be an Internet literate generation. To ensure economic progress and greater opportunity, we must provide an enabling environment. Countries need to prepare and equip themselves to embrace ICT policies. Despite initiatives currently underway and illustrated above, the digital divide is in danger of widening, not closing. In these regards, creative and innovative alliances must be created and dedicated to improving the conditions and prospects of children and youth.

Without the collaboration of governments, international organizations, social movements and the private sector, the Internet is as likely to deepen the gulf between rich and poor as to bridge it. Millions of children and youth will become victims to the digital divide. The Internet should not be considered a panacea for the social inequalities in the developing world, but by taking appropriate measures, we can mitigate the damage. The Internet alone cannot bring an end to the problems that children and youth around the world are facing. Information and communication technologies are only tools that provide powerful resources in the fight against poverty. The final report presented by the DOT Force to leaders at the G8 Summit in Genoa, Italy, in July 2001, contained some "big ideas" to mobilize support and develop ICT projects in the developing world. In order to achieve the goals presented at the Summit, strategic alliance must be constructed and sustained at all levels. The challenge is tremendous and the results remain to be seen, but children and youth around the world must be empowered by the new digital revolution in order to have a better and more productive future.

Chapter 2

Has the Information Age Created a New Economy?

Chapter Preface

The 1990s witnessed one of the longest economic expansions in the history of the United States. According to Dean Baker of the Center for Economic Policy and Research,

> The period from the fourth quarter of 1995 to the end of 2000 was the economy's best sustained economic performance since 1973. . . . Annual productivity growth in this period averaged almost 2.5 percent. This is more than a half percentage point above the rate of productivity growth in the seventies and nearly twice the growth in the eighties. . . . Real wage growth also picked up during this period, with average hourly compensation rising at a real rate of 2.2 percent annually. . . . In addition, the unemployment rate sunk to its lowest point in thirty years, bottoming out at 3.9 percent for several months in 2000.

In the wake of this growth, a remarkable new theory emerged—that the Information Age had created a "New Economy" in which productivity and prosperity would reach unprecedented heights. "It is the proliferation of information technology throughout the economy that makes the current period appear so different from preceding decades," said Federal Reserve chairman Alan Greenspan in July 2000. In this view, e-mail, the World Wide Web, and sophisticated computer software were largely responsible for the prosperity, as businesses harnessed these technologies to improve efficiency and raise profits. Some observers predicted that the New Economy might not be subject to the business cycle—periods of prosperity followed by recessions—that has always plagued the "Old Economy." In December 1999 *Wall Street Journal* reporter Thomas Petzinger Jr. wrote that "The business cycle—a creation of the Industrial Age—may well become an anachronism."

In the "dot-com mania" of 1999–2000, excitement over information technology led many people to invest in newly founded Internet companies that promised to generate enormous profits through e-commerce. The value of technology stocks soared. However, in the spring of 2000, investors began abandoning Internet companies that had not shown a profit, and technology stocks began to fall. Media pundits began to refer to "dot-coms" as "dot-bombs." Some analysts claimed that a "New Economy" had never really existed and that a recession was imminent. "The new economy is just the old economy," wrote *PC Magazine* columnist John C. Dvorak in October 2001. "We're left with an Internet that is a spam-ridden shambles. We have . . . thousands of dead dot-coms, broadband malaise, and a tech industry left in a mess."

Debate over the New Economy rages on, and the viewpoints in the following chapter further explore whether the Information Age has created a New Economy. Ultimately, however, only time will tell if any of the many predictions about the New Economy are accurate.

Information Technology Has Transformed the U.S. Economy

by the Council of Economic Advisors

About the author: The Council of Economic Advisors was established by the Employment Act of 1946 to provide the president with objective economic analysis and advice on the development and implementation of a wide range of domestic and international economic policy issues. The following viewpoint is excerpted from the council's January 2001 report to then President Bill Clinton.

Over the last 8 years [from 1993 to 2000] the American economy has transformed itself so radically that many believe we have witnessed the creation of a New Economy. This [viewpoint] presents evidence of fundamental and unanticipated changes in economic trends that justify this claim. In the 1990s, after two decades of disappointing performance, the economy enjoyed one of its most prosperous periods ever. Strong and rising growth in real gross domestic product (GDP), declining and then very low unemployment, and a low, stable core inflation rate characterize the long expansion. Even though growth moderated in the second half of 2000, the achievements of the past 8 years remain impressive.

From the first quarter of 1993 through the third quarter of 2000, real GDP grew at an average annual rate of 4.0 percent—46 percent faster than the average from 1973 to 1993. This exceptional growth reflects both strong job creation and increased productivity growth. Americans are working in record numbers: the number of payroll jobs has increased by more than 22 million since January 1993, and in 2000 the share of the population employed reached its highest level on record. Also in 2000 the unemployment rate dipped to 3.9 percent, the lowest level in a generation. Unemployment rates for African Americans and Hispanic Americans were the lowest since separate statistics for these groups were first collected in the early 1970s.

Excerpted from *The Annual Report of the Council of Economic Advisors,* by the Council of Economic Advisors (Washington, DC: Government Printing Office, 2001).

Americans are not only working more; they are also working smarter. The economy has rapidly become more productive. Since the beginning of 1993, output per hour in the nonfarm business sector has grown at an average rate of 2.3 percent per year, compared with an average of 1.4 percent per year for the previous 20 years. Even more remarkably, since the fourth quarter of 1995 productivity growth has averaged 3 percent per year. This acceleration in productivity has produced higher incomes and greater wealth. From 1993 to 1999, the real income of the median household grew more than in any period of similar length in the last 30 years. Meanwhile the value of corporate stocks has nearly trebled, even after taking into account the downward adjustment in stock prices during 2000.

These income gains have also been widely shared: even incomes at the bottom of the distribution have risen rapidly. Disadvantaged groups have seen their situation improve markedly. The overall poverty rate declined to 11.8 percent in 1999 (the most recent year for which data are available), its lowest level since 1979 and 3.3 percentage points below the rate in 1993. The poverty rate for African Americans was 23.6 percent in 1999—still too high, but far below the 1993 level of 33.1 percent. The poverty rates for Hispanic Americans and elderly Americans have also fallen sharply. . . .

The Economy from 1973 to 1993

The remarkable economic trends of the 1990s took many by surprise. They represent a distinct change from the 1970s and 1980s, decades in which the economy was plagued by persistent inflation, periodically high unemployment, slow growth in productivity, rising inequality, and large Federal budget deficits. Stagflation was an unwelcome phenomenon of the 1970s, as two major oil shocks were followed by simultaneous inflation and recession. The massive and costly recession of the early 1980s and the collapse of oil prices in 1986 broke the back of the very high inflation rates that had emerged in the late 1970s. But as unemployment fell below 6 percent in the late 1980s, core inflation started to climb again. Between 1973 and 1993, GDP growth received a boost from the large numbers of women and baby-boomers entering the workforce. But at the same time, persistently slow productivity growth (averaging less than half of what it had been during the preceding 25 years) kept GDP growth in check.

"Americans are working in record numbers."

These trends affected the incidence of poverty. In the 1960s and early 1970s, poverty had been declining as economic progress gradually raised the incomes of those at the bottom. The nationwide poverty rate, which had stood at 22.2 percent in 1960, fell to 11.1 percent in 1973. But the combination of slow productivity growth and a relatively slack labor market likely played a role in ending this improvement, dragging down household incomes, especially for the poorest. The poverty rate continued to fluctuate, falling during expansions in the business cycle and rising during contractions. However, throughout the 1980s it never fell lower than 12.8 percent, far above the low of the early 1970s. And by 1993 poverty had risen to 15.1 percent, almost matching the 1983 level of 15.2 percent, its worst since the 1960s.

Federal budget deficits had become commonplace in the 1970s, but they increased rapidly in the 1980s in the presence of a fiscal policy based on overly optimistic budget forecasts. Efforts to restore fiscal discipline in 1990 failed because of a weakening economy, and deficits grew worse rather than better, reaching almost $300 billion in fiscal 1992. By the end of fiscal 1981, publicly held Federal debt had fallen to 25.8 percent of GDP. By the end of fiscal 1993 it had almost doubled, to 49.5 percent.

Given these problems, few believed in 1993 that the U.S. economy could achieve and sustain low unemployment rates, moderate inflation, or robust productivity growth, let alone all three. The Federal Government seemed incapable of balancing its budget, and there was little to suggest that U.S. incomes could grow more rapidly than those in other major industrial countries. Yet in the years that followed, all of these seemingly improbable events occurred—and at the same time.

What Makes the Economy New?

The U.S. economy today displays several exceptional features. The first is its strong rate of productivity growth. Since 1995 the trend rate of productivity growth has been more than double that of the 1973–95 period. A second is its unusually low levels of both inflation and unemployment. In the past, low levels of unemployment have usually meant sharply rising inflation. Yet despite an unemployment rate that has been close to (and at times below) 4 percent for 2 years, core inflation has remained in the 2 to 3 percent range. A third is the disappearance of Federal budget deficits. Federal fiscal policy often becomes more expansionary as a period of economic growth is sustained, yet in the past 8 years the structural budget balance has moved steadily from a massive deficit to a large surplus. A fourth is the strength of the U.S. economy's performance relative to other industrial economies. As a world technological leader, the United States might have been expected to grow more slowly than countries that can benefit from imitating the leader's technological advances. Yet over the second half of the 1990s, the United States continued to enjoy both the highest income per capita and the fastest income growth of the major industrial nations. These developments reveal profound changes in economic trends that justify the term "New Economy."

Three interrelated factors lie behind these extraordinary economic gains: technological innovation, organizational changes in businesses, and public policy. Information technology has long been important to the economy. But in the early 1990s a number of simultaneous advances in information technology—computer hardware, software, and telecommunications—allowed these new technologies to be combined in ways that sharply increased their economic potential.

In part to realize this potential, entrepreneurs instituted widespread changes in business organizations, reconfiguring their existing businesses and starting new ones. These changes included new production methods and human resource management practices, new types of relationships with suppliers and customers, new business strategies (with some firms expanding the scope of their enterprises through mergers and acquisitions, and others streamlining them to best utilize core competencies), and new forms of finance and compensation.

Public policy was the third driving force. This Administration embraced policies and strategies based on fiscal discipline, investing in people and technologies, opening new markets at home and abroad, and developing an institutional framework that supported continued global integration. Together these created an environment in which the new technologies and organizational changes could flourish.

The interactions among these three factors have created a virtuous cycle in which developments in one area reinforce and stimulate developments in another. The result is an economic system in which the whole is greater than the sum of its parts. New technologies have created opportunities for organizational innovations, and these innovations in turn have engendered demand for these technologies and others still newer. The increased

> *"Spending on information technology has clearly played a leading role in the recent acceleration of economic growth."*

growth prompted by the new technologies helped the Federal Government restrain its spending growth and boosted its revenue; the resulting smaller budget deficits (and later surpluses) have helped keep interest rates down, encouraging further investment in new technologies. Economic policies directed toward promoting competition have prodded firms to adopt the new technologies, spurring other firms to innovate or be left behind. Policies aimed at opening foreign markets have increased earnings in the U.S. technology sector, leading to yet more innovation, including innovation in information technologies, which have lowered barriers to trade and investment still further. These market-opening policies have also allowed U.S. producers to become more productive, by expanding the variety of key inputs available to them.

This [viewpoint] defines the New Economy by the extraordinary gains in performance—including rapid productivity growth, rising incomes, low unemployment, and moderate inflation—that have resulted from this combination of mutually reinforcing advances in technologies, business practices, and economic policies. . . .

Spending on information technology has clearly played a leading role in the recent acceleration of economic growth. Although this sector remains a fairly small part of the economy—its share of GDP was an estimated 8.3 percent in 2000—it accounted for almost one-third of all output growth between 1995 and 1999. Even more remarkable, in 1999 business spending on information technology equipment and software was responsible for more than 11 percentage points of the 14 percent real growth in total equipment and software spending by business. The information technology sector is also one that has seen a surge in innovation. To be sure, the computer, the

> *"The excitement over the technology revolution drove technology stocks to extraordinary heights in the spring of 2000."*

cell phone, optical fibers, lasers, and the Internet had all been invented before the mid-1990s. But over the course of that decade, a series of innovations in computer hardware and software and in telecommunications took place that has allowed for new and complementary interactions among these technologies on an unprecedented scale—a dramatic example of which is the emergence and increasing commercial use of the World Wide Web.

There is a broad consensus that information technology has been important in the recent surge in economic performance. But the role of developments beyond this sector remains more controversial. One view of the recent economic transformation identifies the New Economy narrowly with the production and use of information technology. Some proponents of this view argue that performance in the rest of the economy has simply followed previous trends, or that the recent strong economic growth has boosted it only temporarily.

Although the innovation and diffusion of information technology have clearly been important, the broader definition of the New Economy adopted in this [viewpoint] more accurately conveys the pervasiveness of the recent economic changes. A growing body of evidence now shows that the widespread application of information technologies has stimulated remarkable improvements in production processes and other business practices outside the information technology sector. But innovations in information technology and its use have not been the only source of such change. Indeed, there has been a surge in innovation in other technologies as well. Together with supportive public policies, these changes have fundamentally transformed the economy. . . .

Innovations in the Information Technology Sector

The process by which new information technologies are created in the United States has undergone a number of major changes that have transformed the ways in which such innovation occurs. In much of the postwar period, defense spending was a major driver of innovation, and the Federal budget was a more important source of R&D funding than it is today. Innovation, however, was undertaken predominantly by large manufacturers, and the U.S. economy was less integrated with the international economy than it is today.

That situation has changed considerably. . . .

The number of new firms in the information technology sector is a measure of the incentives and opportunity to innovate—and the figures paint a dramatic picture. Between 1990 and 1997 the number of information technology firms more than doubled. Many innovations have come from talented individuals in small startup companies that are willing to take risks. . . .

The excitement over the technology revolution drove technology stocks to extraordinary heights in the spring of 2000, although they have retreated since then. The volatility in technology equity markets can be disruptive to companies seeking new funding, but investors' willingness to take risks and the availability of financial resources for successful entrepreneurs continue to make U.S. financial markets important contributors to the New Economy. Even after the recent decline in the technology sector, price-earnings ratios remain high. This indicates that investors are still willing to take a chance on companies with low current earnings but the potential for rapid future growth.

The changes in the information technology sector have been both cumulative and complementary. Innovations in one area have created demands in another. Breakthroughs in communications and data compression techniques, for instance, generate demand for improved software and for more powerful computers. Complementarities operate on both the supply and the demand sides. In particular, the falling costs associated with the use of computers have made certain types of research feasible for the first time—the mapping of the human genome, for instance, was made feasible by computers. Information technology is becoming increasingly important in the development of new treatment options, and the Food and Drug Administration uses computers to streamline the analysis and approval of new drugs. Demand is particularly powerful when it generates positive feedback through network effects. E-mail, for example, becomes increasingly useful as more people use it. . . .

> *"Companies throughout the U.S. economy have been radically transformed by new technologies."*

Innovation Throughout the Economy

Simply buying and installing new technology does not automatically increase productivity, profitability, or job creation. Yet some views of the New Economy reveal a kind of naïve technological determinism that ignores the vital role of complementary changes in production and business practices. Companies throughout the U.S. economy have been radically transformed by new technologies that enable entire product networks to become more efficient, effective, and integrated. A few of the most important changes are noted here, including changes in production, inventory and supply management, [and] customer relations. . . .

New Production Methods. Innovations in information technology have generated many changes in manufacturing processes. New technologies permit workers to analyze data and make detailed adjustments to production lines on the plant floor, boosting productivity, improving quality, and lowering costs. The availability of data, often on a real-time basis, allows for continuous performance evaluation that can improve efficiency. Workers who have access to information technology can be empowered with more decision-making responsibility. In addition, the new technology allows organizations to disseminate information and coordinate their activities more easily, resulting in less hierarchical organizational structures. In turn, these new structures may reduce costs and further increase efficiency. Finally, as in the information technology sector itself, innovations in the way workers are compensated can help firms achieve greater productivity gains from new technology, spurring further innovation in compensation and finance. Studies suggest that worker performance improves when incentives are tied more closely to performance. Stock options have become more common as a method of attracting, retaining, and rewarding employees.

> *"Information technology has become a pervasive part of economic life, changing the way nearly all Americans work."*

Changes in Inventory and Supply Chain Management. Firms typically hold inventories as a cushion against uncertainties. Producers keep excess raw materials and other inputs on hand to prevent shortages on the production line, for example, and stores maintain inventories to meet fluctuations in demand. The need for inventories springs in part from incomplete information about demand. For this reason, technologies that improve the dissemination of information enable companies to react more promptly to market signals and to economize on inventories (by sharing point-of-sale data, for example). Indeed, aggregate inventory-to-sales ratios have fallen significantly since the early 1990s.

The new information technologies have also changed the nature of relationships between firms and their suppliers. Procurement practices have changed radically, as firms become linked to suppliers through Internet-based business-to-business marketplaces. This capability allows businesses to streamline procurement activities, lower transactions costs, improve the management of supplier relationships, and even engage in collaborative product design. "Just-in-time" delivery, facilitated by a more efficient transportation network including both surface and aviation infrastructure, has been instrumental in allowing firms to reduce inventories and lower costs while continuing to provide essential services to producers and consumers.

New Relationships with Customers. Information technologies give firms the ability to develop richer, more targeted relationships with their customers. Firms are able to tailor marketing and product design more precisely to customer needs. Customers, in turn, are able to find and compare the products that most closely match their preferences. Scanner data from retail stores allow companies to monitor which items are selling and which are not. This information can be transmitted back to manufacturers, who can then adjust their production schedules. This avoids stockouts and surplus inventory. The information from scanners can also be used for marketing. Customers who have purchased outdoor adventure products, for example, can be sent information on related gear or travel opportunities that they may wish to purchase. . . .

A Truly *New* Economy

Economic performance in the last 8 years has been so strong and so qualitatively different from that of the previous two decades that it may seem obvious that a New Economy has emerged. When productivity growth and GDP growth both accelerate sharply, when unemployment and inflation fall to their lowest levels in 30 years, when poverty starts to fall again after years of worsening, and when incomes accelerate across the board, clearly a significant change has occurred.

In addition, the economic transformations described in this [viewpoint] point to a truly *New* Economy. Information technology has become a pervasive part of economic life, changing the way nearly all Americans work—from farmers using the Internet to check a satellite report on soil moisture, to software designers using the latest technology to create a new learning program. Computers have been facilitating change in business systems for some time, but the explosive growth in the production and use of information technology that has taken place in recent years has gone much further. The American economy has been profoundly altered.

Information Technology Will Continue to Fuel Economic Growth

by Robert E. Litan

About the author: *Robert E. Litan is vice president and director of the Economic Studies Program and Cabot Family Chair in Economics at the Brookings Institution, a public policy think tank in Washington, D.C.*

The markets may have soured on Internet start-ups. High-tech oases in countries like Malaysia and India may not lift their countries out of poverty. But all those dot-coms and Silicon Valley dreams never had much to do with the real economic impact of the Internet. The new economy is alive and well.

The death of the dot-coms proves the Internet was overhyped. Don't overreact. Sure, the dot-com stock bubble has burst, helping to cut the market value of stocks traded on the NASDAQ in half. It would be a mistake, however, to extend such stock-market negativity to the economic impact of the Internet itself. After all, no one disputes the transformative impact of the railroad and the automobile even though thousands of such companies that were once in business aren't anymore. Competition winnows out the few firms that are able to survive, ensuring that the benefits of new technology are passed on to consumers.

Changing the Way Business Is Done

But forget about all those start-ups for a minute. New technologies do more than just create new firms and consumer products. They change the way that firms throughout the economy do business. The potential cost savings for firms that take advantage of the Internet are significant, maybe more significant for the main-stays of the old economy than for the nimble little outfits that drove NASDAQ up in the 1990s.

The Internet makes it cheaper to design products remotely; reduces the need for vast inventories; provides a better means to target, communicate with, and service customers; cuts the costs of delivering many services and entertainment; and helps companies remove layers of bureaucratic fat. How much will all this add up to? Consider the impact in the United States alone: A study I am completing with fellow Brookings Institution scholar Alice Rivlin and a team of researchers from major U.S. universities suggests that [by 2006], the Internet may save Americans as much as $200 billion annually. In a roughly $10 trillion economy, this 2 percent savings translates into a potential annual productivity improvement of 0.4 percent. Doesn't sound like much? Think again. If cumulated over 10 years, an annual improvement of 0.4 percent would increase the income of the average American by 4 percent, or roughly $1,600—an amount larger than most of the tax-cut plans bandied about during the 2000 U.S. presidential campaign.

Similar productivity gains are possible, even probable, in other industrialized countries, according to a recent study by the United Nations Conference on Trade and Development (UNCTAD), which suggests a gain of almost 5 percent over the long run. UNCTAD is more pessimistic about the potential gains from the Internet in the developing world, although it is conceivable that the Net will jolt the inefficiencies out of firms in these countries and thus produce even larger cost savings. Already, the Internet is making big inroads in countries like Brazil, where banks are radically changing the way they do business by encouraging more customers to go online. Expect financial institutions elsewhere around the world to follow.

The New Economy Is Not About Dot-Coms

The death of the dot-coms spells the beginning of the end of the New Economy. Wrong again. Do not confuse the dot-coms that sprung up around the world in the last decade (especially those fly-by-night e-tailers) with the new economy, which the Clinton administration's last Economic Report of the President defines as the "extraordinary gains in performance—including rapid productivity growth, rising incomes, low unemployment and moderate inflation—that have resulted from [the] combination of mutually reinforcing advances" in information technology, business practices, and overall economic policy.

The benefits of the Net do not hinge on the survival of any new company that the Net seemingly has created. Think of the dot-coms as the first wave of an amphibious assault on the old economy. Unfortunately,

> *"[By 2006], the Internet may save Americans as much as $200 billion annually."*

the casualties in any first attack are heavy. Take Boo.com, the London-based fashion e-tailer, which, after months of intense prelaunch hype, blew through $125 million of venture capital en route to an unglamorous collapse. But the techniques and footholds these short-lived dot-coms establish pave the way for the heavy artillery to come in behind and rescue the day. As of December 2000, seven of the 10 most popular Web sites in the United States were Internet divisions of offline retailers.

The dot-coms have jolted the traditional manufacturing and service companies of our economy, not only waking them up to the importance of doing business on the Net but also to the sizable opportunities for reducing costs. Outgoing chairman of General Electric Jack Welch has ordered every business line in his company to become Internet-enabled, from the back end of ordering supplies to the front end of dealing with customers. The key will be moving all that once was on paper onto the Internet. Caterpillar, makers of heavy construction equipment (as old economy as it gets), predicts that its new Internet-based electronic marketplace will save the firm $100 million in 2001. Even independent booksellers, once thought by Amazon.com and Barnes & Noble to be roadkill, have joined together to form their own Web site, BookSense.com.

Some dot-coms are expanding or simply avoiding the dot-com slump by partnering with, and modernizing, old-economy firms. Looks.com, the first e-commerce site in Asia for beauty products, couldn't convince cosmetics firms to distribute to a Web-only outfit. Instead of folding, the company merged with Icon, Hong Kong's cosmetics megastore. E*Trade, a thriving Web-based stock-trading service, announced plans to open 200 mini-branches in SuperTarget stores around the United States.

> *"A new and improved old economy is being transformed by the new economy."*

The bottom line? A new and improved old economy is being transformed by the new economy.

We can judge the IT revolution by the numbers. Hardly. Economists spend much time estimating how much the information technology (IT) revolution contributes to economic growth. [In 2000] the U.S. Commerce Department announced that IT industries, though they account for less than 10 percent of the U.S. economy's total output, contributed almost one third of U.S. economic growth between 1995 and 1999. But numbers alone do not fully capture the economic contribution of either the Internet or the broader IT revolution. Many of the benefits of high technology are easy to intuit but hard to quantify.

Consider the convenience of being able to comparison shop and then buy items and services from your living room without driving to multiple stores. The official number crunchers find it hard to put a value on that. Similar difficulties plague attempts to quantify the benefit of being able to customize purchases so easily, as I did when I ordered the Dell computer on which this article was written. Simply put, there are no "markets" for convenience and customization that permit official statisticians to value them in the nation's figures for total output.

What about the fact that in the near future, the Net will even save lives? No longer will pharmacists have to decipher the illegible handwriting of doctors ordering drug prescriptions, which studies confirm has contributed to needless deaths and suffering; instead, doctors will soon transmit prescriptions from handheld computers directly to pharmacies. Not only will such technology save lives, it will make medicine more cost-effective. But none of this will show up in the gross domestic product (GDP) statistics.

The Global New Economy

Silicon Valley can be replicated around the world. It's possible. Not likely, but possible. Silicon Valley has become the economic Mecca of the United States. Foreign business and government leaders—and even mayors and business leaders of other cities in the United States—have trooped to the valley in search of finding the magic elixir to bottle and take back home in hopes of replicating the valley's economic miracle.

Sometimes it works. Bangalore, India, has become famous for supplying software engineers to computer centers around the world. The Tel Aviv–Haifa corridor in Israel has been a magnet for U.S. high-tech companies and a breeding ground for successful new Israeli software and Internet appliance companies. Both Finland and Sweden have become known for their prowess in wireless technologies, as has Japan for its DoCoMo wireless Internet technology. Hsinchu Park in Taiwan has become world-famous for its computer manufacturing. Even tiny Ireland has become a high-tech haven in Europe.

It is easier to identify the keys to high-tech success, however, than to replicate it. The basic ingredients? Well-developed communications infrastructure; a large pool of skilled workers, produced either by local universities that are on the cutting-edge of technology (such as in India) or by multinational companies that have been welcomed with open arms (in Ireland and Israel, for instance); an environment that encourages new business formation; and, at least for those regions that specialize in computer software and Internet-related activities, workers who are fluent in English, the language of roughly 80 percent of all Web pages.

Adding these ingredients to a more general menu of secure property rights and sound fiscal and monetary policy is a recipe for economic success in the 21st century whether or not the intention is to create another Silicon Valley. Foreign investment, and with it ideas and managerial talent, will flow to countries with educated workforces, modern communications, and secure property rights. So will venture capital.

But will such investment radically transform a country's economy and work culture, as Silicon Valley has done in the United States? Whether success in the high-tech sector alone produces noticeable economy-wide gains depends heavily on the size of the country. In large countries like India, building a successful high-tech industry is like throwing a pebble into an ocean: There is scant evidence that the high earners in Bangalore have done much to help reduce widespread poverty elsewhere in the country. In fact, software companies only employ about 340,000 of the country's 1 billion people; 50 percent of the population, meanwhile, is illiterate. China is a better model for other large countries: By educating its masses of children to use modern technologies, it should be able to deliver the gains promised by IT throughout the population.

Meanwhile, in smaller countries like Ireland and Israel, success of a key sector like high tech can produce economic gains that are felt throughout much of the economy. In Ireland, the high-tech boom of the 1990s coincided with an 8 percent annual increase in economic growth between 1993 and 1998 and a decrease in unemployment from 20 percent to 5 percent.

Losers in the New Economy

The IT revolution will worsen the distribution of income. For a time, yes. In the early 1990s, Princeton economist Alan Krueger found that Americans with computer skills earned about 10 percent more than those without them. The computer wage premium in industrialized, democratic nations should gradually fall, however, as computer education spreads throughout the school-age population and the workforce, as more computer-literate professionals emigrate from abroad, and as the penetration rates of PCs and cheaper Internet access continue to increase.

But it is hard to be as optimistic about the growing income gaps between rich Western countries and the developing world, where people are lucky to hook up to a telephone, let alone the Internet. India, frequently hailed as a high-tech success story, has only 15 telephone lines and two computers for every 1,000 citizens. It is possible that the diffusion of wireless phones will help close the gap, but even that will take time and offers no guarantees. The World Bank estimates that just establishing adequate IT infrastructure in developing countries would require a $300 billion investment. Remember, one third of the world's population does not even have electricity.

Developing countries will continue to fall behind unless they take some aggressive steps. Start with telecom reform. Charges for accessing local networks must be brought in line with costs, while customers should be charged a flat local rate that does not vary with the length of time they spend on the phone or online. Had flat-rate pricing not been available in the United States, the Internet never would have taken off as it did; just look at IT giant Japan, where a near monopoly by Nippon Telegraph and Telephone Company and per-minute charges for local calls mean less than a quarter of Japanese use the Internet, compared with half of all Americans. Plus, there are creative ways to wire a country. Private-sector architects of the Barangay Payphone Program in the Philippines are installing pay phones in areas underserved by regular telephone infrastructure and building telecenters (each with a PC, scanner, printer, and Internet connection) in every one of the country's 1,500 municipalities.

> *"Many of the benefits of high technology are easy to intuit but hard to quantify."*

But accessing the Internet is not enough. Governments must make major efforts to provide computer training, not just for the current school population but for adult workers as well. One way to accomplish the latter is to welcome foreign companies that can help train local workforces (as they are doing in Ireland and India) and thus match the physical capital required for the Internet age with its human counterparts.

Regulating the New Economy

Regulation will undermine the global growth of e-commerce. Not likely. During the early years of the Net, cyberliberatarians hailed it as the only "space" in the world that was free from government intervention: no taxes, no regulation, no government! What could be better?

Not surprisingly, governments around the world have not been as overjoyed. Authoritarian leaders understandably view the Internet as a threat, a vehicle for importing subversive ideas, pornography, and other unwelcome content. Similar concerns have arisen in democratic societies, along with worries that the Net will undermine tax revenues, further erode personal privacy, and threaten the legal protection of music, videos, and other Web-based content.

> *"In smaller countries like Ireland and Israel, success of a key sector like high tech can produce economic gains that are felt throughout much of the economy."*

Governments are gradually starting to regulate the Net, encouraged in some cases by citizens who fear its downsides and in others by businesses that simply want some clear rules. The European Union (EU) has imposed new, sweeping privacy protections, both on- and offline, and for a time appeared ready to force the United States to do the same. In the end, the EU accepted self-regulation by U.S. companies, provided that the U.S. Federal Trade Commission punish failures to honor promises to safeguard information. In the United States, Congress has enacted a law giving legal effect to "digital signatures," contracts signed and sealed over the Internet, while prohibiting states and localities from imposing any "new" taxes on Internet transactions. . . .

Perhaps the most contentious issue is government censorship of the Net, a practice employed not only by China and Singapore but most recently by France, where a court required Yahoo to block French users from accessing Nazi material. The French ruling, perhaps more than any other by a liberal democracy, has generated fears that government regulation will become increasingly ambitious until it disrupts global Internet commerce.

The fears are justified but also must be put in some perspective. No one really knows how much money cross-border Internet commerce currently generates. The few official statistics that are available track e-commerce within countries, not between them. And even these data show that e-commerce is hardly overwhelming: about $20 billion in retail e-commerce and perhaps $100 billion in business-to-business e-commerce in the United States in 1999, a year in which total U.S. GDP was about $9 trillion.

The real question is whether some kind of international collective action will be necessary to ensure that various national regulations do not artificially choke global Internet commerce in the future. The opportunities for conflict are abundant, from taxation and rules for intellectual property to privacy, customs, rules for telecommunications services, and even the ownership of Internet domain names. There has been non-governmental international coordination of domain names by the Internet Corporation for Assigned Names and Numbers, but its long-term future is cloudy without assurances of long-term funding.

Probably, over time international rules will slowly emerge in many, if not most, of these areas. In the meantime, efforts by individual countries to wall themselves off from the Net will almost certainly backfire. Why? Overregulating countries, their firms, and their citizens will simply find themselves bypassed by the Internet revolution—not a welcome prospect.

The Internet Has Not Created a New Economy

by Dwight R. Lee

About the author: *Dwight R. Lee is a professor of economics in the Terry College of Business at the University of Georgia.*

The Internet is clearly a marvelous technological advance, allowing hundreds of millions of people from all over the globe to exchange information almost instantly. But the claims that it is creating a new economy based on information and communication are pure hype. Long before the Internet we were benefiting from an amazing network of global communication and information in the old free-market economy. There is nothing new about an "information economy."

Market economies have always been information economies. The Internet can improve the information transmitted through markets, but that information has always been the reason for the amazing success of free-market economies. Let's admire the Internet for the marginal improvements it makes to our market economy. But while admiring the shine let's not ignore the shoe.

The Market Network

Every day each of us simultaneously exchanges messages with millions upon millions of people through the market network. The information we transmit is picked up quickly by those who can best use it, informs them on the appropriate action to take, and provides them the means and motivation to take that action.

The result is a pattern of global cooperation that finds each of us serving the interests of millions of others by using our time and talents to provide what they value most, while benefiting from their reciprocal consideration. This market network has been enriching the lives of those people lucky enough to live in free economies long before the advent of the Internet.

Communication in the market network takes place through prices based on private property and voluntary exchange. Private property is essential for people to engage in voluntary exchange, and when exchange is voluntary it typically takes place at a price that reflects the highest value of what is being exchanged (people generally sell to those willing to pay the most).

So market prices communicate the value others place on the things we own, and motivate us to relinquish those things to others when they are worth more to them than to us. Similarly, market prices for goods and services also reflect the costs of making them available. People will not consistently sell a product at a price less than the value sacrificed to make it available.

So market prices communicate how much value is given up elsewhere in the economy to provide products, and motivates us to buy products only when the additional unit is worth more to us than the sacrifice our purchases impose on others.

Firms are constantly listening to the market messages of consumers that are sent in the form of profits and losses. Consumers inform firms with profits when those firms are using resources to produce more value than those resources are producing in other activities, and they respond by expanding their production. On the other hand, consumers inform other firms with losses that they are not providing enough value to cover their cost, and those firms respond by producing less.

> *"There is nothing new about an 'information economy.'"*

I'm not arguing that market prices are the best form of communication for all occasions. How do you say "I Love You" with a market price? Very clumsily. But market prices are far and away the most persuasive way to communicate your desire for chocolates and roses, which will increase the impact of—and payoff from—saying "I Love You."

An Improvement, Not a Transformation

Of course, the Internet has made it easier to order those chocolates and roses, but it's the incentives provided by market prices that insure the cooperation of the literally thousands of people who have to coordinate their efforts to get them to you when and where you need them.

Let's give the Internet credit. It is making important changes in our lives and the way we do business. Certainly the Internet is improving market communication in important ways. But without the market network we would all be impoverished by our inability to communicate and cooperate with the millions of people we depend on everyday, no matter how much access we had to the Internet.

The New Economy Is No Different than the Old Economy

by Paul Wallace

About the author: *Paul Wallace is a former economics editor for the British newspaper* Independent *and a frequent contributor to the* New Statesman, *a magazine published in the United Kingdom.*

You may think that whoever coined the name Oxygen for the latest soar-away Internet company must have had a sense of humour. The financial bubble in dot com stocks is hardly short of air. But it is just as likely that Oxygen Holdings' twentysomething venture capitalists—whose ritzy media backers include Matthew Freud and Elisabeth Murdoch—don't see the joke at all. After all, they're incubating (nothing so mundane as investing in) start-ups in the new e-economy of virtual value and endless boom. Financial bubbles are a fuddy-duddy discredited old economy idea.

Yet we are not so much charting new territory as warping back to the globalised economy of the 19th century. The Victorian era holds up a mirror to the present day that is far more revealing—and sobering—than the crystal ball of our Panglossian futurologists.

Comparing the New Economy with the Old

To listen to new economy hypesters—let's call them the neweconomistas—you would imagine that global communication and delivery had been invented yesterday. No doubt they are too busy boning up on e-jargon and brainstorming hip domain-names to recall J M Keynes's description of the world around 1900: "The inhabitant of London could order by telephone, sipping his morning tea in bed, the various products of the whole earth and reasonably expect their early delivery upon his doorstep; he could at the same moment and by the same means adventure his wealth in the natural resources and new enterprises of any quarter of the world, and share, without exertion or even trouble, in their prospective fruits and advantages."

One-click ordering may now have jazzy shopping trolley icons, but it's still home delivery. That's old, not new. E-mail may be a hundred times superior to snail-mail, but Amazon still delivers your books by post or courier. Ordering your groceries from the local Tesco's doesn't sound so far removed from ringing up the village store and getting them sent round in the van.

Even so, let us accept that e-commerce is opening up a new electronic frontier, one that slashes distribution costs and empowers consumers. Does this amount to an unprecedented economic revolution? Only to those who never watch Westerns.

In 1850, the US had less than 10,000 miles of railroads; by 1910, this had risen to 250,000. Steam replaced sail. Transportation costs nosedived, making it possible to buy foodstuffs and commodities on the world market. The consequence: a dramatic international price convergence, argue Kevin O'Rourke and Jeffrey Williamson in *Globalisation and History*. In 1870, wheat in Liverpool was three-fifths more expensive than in Chicago; 25 years later, the margin had fallen to less than a fifth. An even bigger price gap for meat in 1895 collapsed in the next 15 years, as refrigeration made the British market accessible to faraway foreign imports.

So today's electronic revolution gives us a welcome advance, but hardly an unprecedented change. Time for the neweconomistas to shift ground—to the claim that the Internet economy is wholly new in its potential to make information instantly available to all. In financial markets, for example, day-traders, glued to computers in their back-bedrooms, are taking over from old-style professional dealers.

But all advances are relative. Before the first transatlantic cable was laid in 1866, information in the City of London about prices on Wall Street was three weeks out of date. The cable gave traders current prices within the day. Price differences between London and New York fell by over two-thirds. Moving from weeks to a day is a bigger advance than moving from telephone to Internet trading.

There are further striking parallels between today's "new" economy and the old economy of the 19th century. Over the past two decades, capital has broken free from national boundaries. Last year, companies' foreign

> *"One-click ordering may now have jazzy shopping trolley icons, but it's still home delivery. That's old, not new."*

direct investment reached a record $800 billion. Yet before the first world war, capital was also on the move, and on an even more astounding scale in relation to the size of economies. At its peak, Britain's foreign investment accounted for almost a tenth of output or a half of total savings. The big difference between today and the 19th century is that, though capital can now move freely, it's not so easy for people. It's true that there is more migration now than in most of the rest of the 20th century; but, generally, you are better off as a can of beans if you want to move to another country.

The new economy combines low inflation and low unemployment—not the sort of mix you're supposed to have in the dismal trade-offs of the dismal science. Neweconomistas frequently attribute the death of inflation to the high-tech revolution. But inflation has been in retreat since the mid 1970s. It fell substantially in the 1990s before the Internet flourished.

Again the parallel with the late 19th century is instructive. Then, prices fell as domestic markets opened up to international competition. British farmers were hammered by cheap producers in the new world. Today, vast new industrial capacity has come on stream in Asia. Firms are losing the pricing power they could once exert in national economies; this in turn keeps wage pressures at bay.

But what makes the e-economy year zero for its over-excited cheerleaders is the impact of Information Technology (IT) and the Internet on productivity. Inspired by a recent surge in American productivity figures, the neweconomistas envisage a permanent improvement in the growth of output per worker. Recent productivity gains are certainly impressive compared with America's recent past. They are comparable, however, to those in Japan or the UK in the late 1980s and, as economists at HSBC observe: "We all know what happened to those two 'new

> *"There are ... striking parallels between today's 'new' economy and the old economy of the 19th century."*

paradigm' models as they entered the 1990s." Indeed, productivity growth has recently been falling in both the UK and the euro zone.

The point about America is that when economies operate beyond full capacity, as in the US today, productivity figures flatter to deceive. More output is squeezed out of the labour force than is sustainable in the long run. The truth is revealed when the economy slows down or goes into decline in the down-leg of the business cycle.

The business cycle? But my dear, that's so old economy. With the US celebrating its longest expansion in history, the business cycle has been written out of the script.

A Recession Is Inevitable

This is a triumph of wishful thinking over experience. The business cycles of the 19th century were driven, like the current upswing, by investment rather than by consumer or government spending. In principle, investment is a good thing. But you can have too much of a good thing, especially when investment is spurred by soaring stock markets. As Keynes wrote: "There is an inducement to spend on a new project what may seem an extravagant sum, if it can be floated off on the stock exchange at an immediate profit." Only when the financial climate turns sour is the new project revealed as a waste of money. That's when the music ends and the debts (in hard cash) are no longer dwarfed by soaring valuations of paper assets.

The characteristic rhythm of the 19th-century business cycle was a long investment-driven upswing that often topped out in a speculative mania. A sharp recession followed. So far, we have not encountered a similar downside, but it is surely waiting in the wings. As Walter Bagehot wrote more than a century ago: "At particular times a great deal of stupid people have a great deal of stupid money." Ring a bell? Today's stupid people may no longer be Bagehot's "quiet ladies, rural clergymen and country misers", but their money is just as stupid, their capital just as blind. An old rule of thumb was to move out of stocks when the cab driver bent your ear with his latest stockpicking prowess. By this token, when the Mirror's tipster column stops delivering the news and becomes the news, it's time to take cover.

Whenever shares rise—or fall—there is never any shortage of storytellers to explain why. The agreed story line on Internet stocks is that the new virtual economy is rapidly displacing the old industrial economy. Buy that (and the shares) if you like—but don't forget that capitalism has always been about creative destruction. A more plausible interpretation is that this is an old-fashioned gold rush—another disconcerting echo of the 19th century. And what happened at these Klondikes? A few prospectors hit gold, while the rest panned for fool's gold. It's the same with Internet companies. A very few genuinely innovative players like Yahoo! have broken into the rich seam of eyeball count that makes for potentially big profits. The rest—the imitative stragglers—are already falling by the wayside.

Does it matter if investors waste their money in speculative blow-outs on companies with wacky names? Unfortunately, yes. When the bubble bursts, there is credit revulsion—to use the evocative Victorian phrase—which affects sound companies as well as back-of-the-envelope ones. Debts that seemed manageable when financial assets were rising become onerous for both consumers and companies. These bad debts have to be purged from the economic system—something that it has taken the Japanese a decade to deal with after their bubble of the 1980s.

Let Keynes—no ivory tower economist but a highly practised investor—have the last word. "Speculators may do no harm as bubbles on a steady stream of enterprise. But the position is serious when enterprise becomes the bubble on a whirlpool of speculation. When the capital development of a country becomes a by-product of the activities of a casino, the job is likely to be ill-done." Oxygen or no oxygen, the Internet bubble will burst and with it more than the naive hopes for a new economy.

Many Claims About the New Economy Have Been Exaggerated

by the *Economist*

About the author: *The* Economist *is a weekly magazine of business and politics.*

The announcement on May 8th [2001] that America's productivity declined in the first quarter of 2001 at an annual rate of 0.1%, compared with growth of more than 5% during the year to June 2000, is a blow for the information technology (IT)-powered new economy. One by one, its claims to be special are being exposed as myths. Now it seems that the widely-held belief that America's sustainable rate of productivity growth had doubled to around 3% was also mere myth. That does not mean, however, that the new economy was entirely hot air.

Its cheerleaders have certainly been muffled this year by the plunge in the Nasdaq high-tech stockmarket index, by the collapse of dotcom firms, by the slump in the profits of Internet giants such as Cisco (which this week reported its first quarterly loss in 11 years and a 30% decline in sales), and by signs that the American economy may be heading into recession. The new-economy sceptics, who long argued that computers and the Internet did not rate in the same economic league as electricity or the car, are now grinning smugly. They have a long list of unfulfilled promises to point to.

Five Myths of the New Economy

The cycle. Top of the list is the idea that the traditional business cycle is dead. Now that America's economy is slowing sharply and unemployment is rising, everybody is trying to deny that they ever made such a claim. Instead, they argue that IT helps to smooth the cycle. But even that claim looks suspect: if America's Gross Domestic Product (GDP) growth this year slows to the average forecast of 1.5%, then the decline in growth from 5% last year would be very abrupt indeed. And because of the excesses that have built up during the boom years—such as too much investment and too little saving—there is a high risk that the downturn could be much deeper. If America's GDP growth were to fall below 1% this year, it would be the sharpest slowdown between any two years since the 1974–75 oil crisis. So much for smoothing.

Inventories. One reason why IT was supposed to smooth out the economic cycle was that fancy computer systems and instant information would allow firms to ensure that production never got too far ahead of sales, and would thus avoid an excessive build-up of inventories. Yet despite spending millions on cutting-edge software, firms failed to spot the slowdown late last year, and now they have warehouses bulging with unwanted stocks. Cisco was supposed to be the very model of modern electronic business, using the Internet to make sales, order components and monitor inventories. But it, too, has been badly caught out. The firm was forced to write down $2.2 billion-worth of excess stocks in the three months to April—equivalent to almost 50% of its sales during the period.

Across the economy as a whole, "just-in-time" inventory management has reduced the ratio of inventories to sales. But it cannot guard against excessive stocks when shocks occur. It can only ensure that for any given shock, the error is smaller than it would otherwise have been. So far, the build-up in stocks is modest given how sharply demand has fallen. But it is far from negligible.

Investment. The third myth of the new economy was that IT spending was recession-proof. Demand for IT equipment, it was argued, would continue to grow briskly throughout any downturn in the old economy because the pace of innovation was so fast that existing IT equipment would rapidly become obsolete. Firms would be forced to keep investing merely to stay competitive.

In reality, as profits have fallen, firms have decided that they can easily delay buying new PCs or upgrading their e-mail systems. In the first quarter of this year, investment in IT equipment and software in America fell at an annual rate of 6.5% in real terms, after rising at an average annual rate of 25% during the period 1995 to 2000. New orders for electronic goods fell at an annualised rate of almost 20% in the first quarter, signalling that bigger cuts are in the pipeline.

Profits. Myth number four was that corporate profits would continue to rise rapidly for years to come. Average profits now look set to fall by at least 10% in 2001. Late last year, equity analysts were forecasting average long-term profits growth of 19%.

> *"The new-economy sceptics . . . are now grinning smugly."*

That has now been revised down to 12%, but it still looks far too optimistic. It implies that profits will account for an ever-rising share of GDP. Yet historically, profits have tended to increase broadly in line with nominal GDP. If anything, the ratio of profits to GDP should now be falling slightly, because IT is likely to trim profit margins by increasing price transparency and shifting power from sellers to buyers.

Share prices. The fifth (and silliest) claim was that in this new world of rapid technological change, old methods of share valuation had become irrelevant. Profits were for wimps, it claimed. Falls of 90–100% in the share prices of loss-making dotcom firms show that profits do matter after all. During previous technological revolutions (spurred by the invention of the railways, electricity or the automobile, for example) share prices similarly soared and then tumbled. But this time prices rose to a higher level in relation to profits than ever before in history.

A Long-Term Boost to Productivity?

What about the most important claim of the new economy, namely that investment in IT has lifted productivity growth? The fall in productivity this year appears to confirm that this was also a myth. But America's productivity gains cannot be dismissed so easily. Recent estimates of sustainable productivity growth were almost certainly too optimistic, but there is still reason to believe that some of the productivity gains will survive even as the IT boom turns to bust.

Labour productivity growth in America's non-farm business sector rose to an annual average of almost 3% over the five years to 2000, up from 1.4% between 1975 and 1995. This faster productivity growth has been the lifeblood of claims about the new economy. It helped to deliver faster GDP growth with low inflation, higher profits and a large budget surplus.

> *"Myth number four was that corporate profits would continue to rise rapidly for years to come."*

One of the hottest debates in economics for the past few years has been about how much of this increase in productivity growth was structural and how much of it was cyclical. During boom times firms tend to work their employees harder, producing a cyclical rise in productivity growth, which then declines during the subsequent recession.

Robert Gordon, an economist at America's Northwestern University, and one of the most outspoken new-economy sceptics, reckons that outside the manufacture of computers and other durable goods there has been no increase in labour productivity growth after adjusting for the effects of the economic cycle. As a result, he estimated last year that America's structural productivity growth was somewhere around 2%.

At the other extreme, two studies published early this year—one by the president's Council of Economic Advisers and the other by the Federal Reserve— both conclude that virtually all the increase in labour productivity growth since 1995 has been structural, putting the sustainable rate at close to 3%.

It is hard to believe that none of the increase in productivity growth was cyclical, given the strength of the recent economic boom. On the other hand, microeconomic studies appear to confirm that a sizeable chunk of the increase has been structural. A study by Kevin Stiroh, an economist at the Federal Reserve

Bank of New York, examined productivity growth in individual industries. Mr Stiroh found that those industries which invested most in IT in the early 1990s saw the biggest productivity gains in the late 1990s. If the increase in productivity growth had been largely cyclical, the gains should have been more equally spread across industries.

> *"The IT investment boom was unsustainable."*

By late last year, as the reported productivity growth figures looked stronger and stronger, a consensus emerged among most economists, including those at America's Federal Reserve and the OECD, that America's structural rate of productivity growth had increased to around 3%.

By itself, the fall in productivity in the first quarter sheds little new light on the issue because quarterly figures tend to jump about a lot. Also, productivity growth always dips as growth slows because firms delay cutting jobs—although the sharp rise in joblessness in America last month suggests that employers there are now wielding the axe. Productivity has held up quite well so far compared with previous downturns: it is still 2.8% higher than a year ago. But we need to wait for a full economic cycle to get the complete picture.

From Boom to Bust

If the fall in productivity growth over the past year is only cyclical (and due to weaker demand) then, once the economy recovers, productivity growth should resume its faster trend. What is becoming increasingly clear, however, is that the productivity gains in recent years were not only exaggerated by the cyclical impact of the economic boom, they were also inflated by an unsustainable IT investment boom that has now turned to bust.

Investing in IT can increase labour productivity either by increasing the amount of capital employed per worker (ie, "capital deepening") or by speeding up total factor productivity (TFP—the efficiency with which both capital and labour are used). Unlike previous spurts in America's productivity growth, the recent one has been unusually dependent on capital deepening rather than on TFP. A study last year, by Stephen Oliner and Daniel Sichel at the Federal Reserve, concluded that almost half of the acceleration in productivity growth between the first and second halves of the 1990s was due to capital deepening. If that is so, a decline in IT investment will have worrying implications for future productivity growth.

The IT investment boom was unsustainable. The initial rise in productivity growth during the 1990s generated bumper profits, which encouraged firms to become over-optimistic about future returns. At the same time, the stockmarket bubble pushed capital costs down to virtually zero. The inevitable result was over-investment. Credit Suisse First Boston (CSFB) estimates that American firms have overspent on IT equipment to the tune of $190 billion over the past two years.

Now, as profits plunge, firms are being forced to cut their investment plans. CSFB suggests that if firms try to eliminate the surplus over two years, real IT investment will need to fall by an average of 16% this year and next. If firms try to extend the life of their existing IT equipment during the downturn, then new investment would have to fall by even more.

One year's dip in investment would have only a modest impact on structural productivity growth if capital spending were then to bounce back strongly. More important is the longer-term trend in investment. America's business capital stock has recently been growing at a real annual rate of over 5%, well in excess of the growth in GDP. Jan Hatzius, an economist at Goldman Sachs, estimates that the trend growth in the capital stock will now slow to 3–3.5%. If so, estimates Mr Hatzius, the contribution of capital deepening to labour productivity growth will be reduced to 0.75%, half its recent rate.

Mr Hatzius also expects the growth in total factor productivity to slow as the cyclical boost to productivity fades, and as efficiency gains in computer manufacturing diminish. One measure of the latter is the pace of price deflation for IT equipment. Price deflation accelerated in the late 1990s, partly because of increased competition and partly because of increased efficiency in the manufacture of chips. But it has since slowed. Computer prices fell by 16% in the year to the end of March, down from an average annual decline of 25% in the previous five years.

Technological Innovation Does Spur Productivity

Putting all this together, Goldman Sachs has reduced its estimate of underlying productivity growth to a more modest 2.25%. That would be barely half the rate of productivity growth in 2000, but it would still be significantly higher than the 1.4% average annual rate recorded between 1975 and 1995. Only if investment stagnated for several years would productivity growth revert to its pre-1995 pace.

And that seems unlikely. The IT boom was mainly driven by falling IT prices that were following Moore's law, which states that the processing power of a silicon chip roughly doubles every 18 months. This encouraged firms to substitute IT equipment for labour or other capital. Scientists believe that Moore's law should hold for at least another ten years, allowing IT prices to continue to fall and hence encouraging further IT capital deepening, albeit at a slower pace than in recent years.

"High-tech investment and productivity growth are . . . unlikely to return to the giddy pace of the past two years [1999–2000]."

Not only is the pace of technological innovation likely to continue to support productivity growth for at least another decade, but firms have yet to exploit fully the potential of their existing IT. It is not just the direct impact of computers and the Internet on productivity that matters, but also the ability of firms to organise their businesses more efficiently as a result. Just as the steam age moved production from the household to the factory, railways allowed the development of mass markets, and electricity made possible the assembly line, so IT allows for a more efficient business organisation.

Tossing aside all the hype, there are sound reasons for expecting IT to continue to boost productivity. By increasing access to information, it helps to make markets work more efficiently and it reduces transaction costs. Better-informed markets should ensure that resources are allocated to their most productive use. The most important aspect of the new economy was never the shift to high-tech industries; it was the way in which IT could improve the efficiency of old-economy firms.

A study by Alice Rivlin and Robert Litan at the Brookings Institution, a Washington think-tank, considers ways in which the Internet might further lift productivity growth. It examines how leading-edge firms are using the Internet to reduce transaction costs, to boost the efficiency of supply-chain management, and to improve communications with customers and suppliers. It then projects best practice across each sector.

The study's tentative conclusion is that the economy as a whole can look forward to productivity gains from the Internet of 0.2–0.4% a year for the next five years. The potential cost savings look especially large in the health-care industry, where there is plenty of scope to improve the management of medical records and to communicate better with patients. Only 3% of Americans have so far corresponded with their doctor by e-mail; the rest still use more time-consuming methods, such as the telephone or a personal visit.

It is also worth remembering that not all of America's productivity growth in recent years has come from IT. Some of it has been the pay-off from earlier economic deregulation designed to make labour, product and capital markets work more efficiently. Whatever happens to IT spending, these benefits will endure.

Modest Predictions

High-tech investment and productivity growth are, however, unlikely to return to the giddy pace of the past two years. The best guess is that productivity growth will average 2–2.5% per year over the next decade, still well above the pace of the 1970s and 1980s. Those who claimed that 3–3.5% growth was sustainable will be disappointed, but their expectations were far too bold. They implied that IT would have a much bigger economic impact than cars and electricity did in the 1920s, when annual labour productivity growth in the non-farm business sector averaged 2.5%.

Slower-than-expected growth in productivity has two implications for policy-makers, however. First, after taking account of labour-market changes, it means the rate at which the Fed can safely allow the economy to grow without pushing up inflation is 3–3.5%, much less than in recent years. Second, it implies a smaller budget surplus—and hence less room for tax cuts. Back-of-the-envelope calculations by Goldman Sachs suggest that if productivity growth falls to 2.25%, the cumulative budget surplus in the years 2002–11 would fall to just over $2 trillion, as against the $3.1 trillion estimated by the Congressional Budget Office.

In recent years, economists have tended to exaggerate about IT. Either they have denied that anything has changed, or they have insisted that everything has changed. The truth, as ever, lay somewhere in the middle.

Future productivity gains from computers and the Internet will probably not be enough to justify current share prices, even after this year's slide, but they will still matter. An increase in productivity growth of 0.5–1.0 percentage points per annum may not sound very exciting, but it will lift future living standards and make it easier for the government to pay tomorrow's pensions. That, rather than the get-rich-quick culture of the dotcoms, is the true stuff of the new economy.

Chapter 3

How Should Governments Respond to the Information Age?

Regulating the Internet: An Overview

by the *Economist*

About the author: *The* Economist *is a weekly magazine of business and politics.*

In 1967 Roy Bates, a retired British army major, occupied an island fortress six miles off the English coast and declared it a sovereign nation. He was never sure what to do with his Principality of Sealand. Now, however, the fortress may have found its calling. For several months, a firm called HavenCo has been operating a data centre there. Anyone who wants to keep a website or other data out of the reach of national governments can rent space on the servers that hum in one of the concrete pillars.

In the mid-1990s, Sealand would have been seen as yet more proof that the Internet cannot be regulated. If a country tried to censor digital content, the data would simply hop to a more liberal jurisdiction. These days, the data principality symbolises just the opposite: the days of unrestricted freedom on the Internet are numbered, except, perhaps, in odd places like Sealand.

It seems likely that 2000 will be remembered as the year when governments started to regulate cyberspace in earnest; and forgot, in the process, that the reason the worldwide network became such an innovative force at all was a healthy mix of self-regulation and no regulation. In Britain, the Regulation of Investigatory Powers Act now gives the police broad access to e-mail and other online communications. South Korea has outlawed access to gambling websites. The United States has passed a law requiring schools and libraries that receive federal funds for Internet connections to install software on their computers to block material harmful to the young.

Governments Grapple with the Information Revolution

This year [2001], governments are turning their attention to the many jurisdictional problems created by the Internet. These have been emphasised by a French ruling against Yahoo! on November 20th. The French court ordered the

Internet portal firm to find some way of banning French users from seeing the Nazi memorabilia posted on its American sites, or face a daily fine of FFr100,000 ($13,000) from the end of February. Yahoo! is fighting the case, even though it has now stopped sales of Nazi memorabilia.

The case could be a taste of things to come. Under a new European Union (EU) law, for example, European consumers may now sue EU-based Internet sites in their own countries, and the rule may well be extended internationally. The United States has just endorsed the gist of the Council of Europe's cyber-crime treaty, which aims to harmonise laws against hacking, Internet fraud and child pornography.

All this is a far cry from what leading Internet thinkers prophesied only five years ago. "You [governments] have no moral right to rule us nor do you possess any methods of enforcement we have true reason to fear," proclaimed John Perry Barlow in his 1996 "Declaration of Independence of cyberspace". Libertarian thinking also ran through early Internet scholarship. David Post and David Johnson, law professors at Temple University in Philadelphia and Georgetown University respectively, argued in that same year that cyberspace was a distinct place that needed laws and legal institutions entirely of its own.

To treat cyberspace differently seemed logical. Because data are sent around the Internet in small packets, each of which can take a different route, the flow of information is hard to stop, even if much of the network is destroyed. It was this built-in resilience that appealed to the Internet's original sponsor, America's Defence Department, and made it the medium of choice for civil libertarians. "The Internet", runs their favourite motto, "interprets censorship as damage and routes around it."

> *"2000 will be remembered as the year when governments started to regulate cyberspace."*

Many online experts argue that, since the Internet does away with geographical boundaries, it also does away with territorially based laws. The transmission of data is almost instant, regardless of where sender and receiver are. Today individuals, as well as multinational companies, can decide in which country to base their websites, thus creating competition between jurisdictions. For example, the United States, thanks to its constitutional guarantee of the right to free speech, has become a safe haven for hundreds of German neo-Nazi sites that are illegal under German law.

Technologies to Tame the Internet

Yet, for all that, governments are not completely helpless in cyberspace. They have some potentially powerful tools at their disposal. Filtering is one. Software installed on a PC, in an Internet service provider's equipment or in gateways that link one country with the rest of the online world, can block access to certain sites.

Less well known, but potentially more important, is the fact that websites themselves can block users. They do so by employing the same technology that serves up tailored banner advertisements to visitors from another country. They track the Internet service provider's "IP address", the number that identifies computers on the Internet and, in many cases, reveals where a user is.

This technology was the basis for the French ruling against Yahoo! The firm had argued that it was technically impossible to prevent French users from reaching auctions of illegal Nazi memorabilia on its sites. But a panel of three technical experts argued that IP-address tracking could spot more than 60% of French surfers.

> *"Filtering and identification technologies will help to make cyberspace more regulated."*

Both filtering and IP-address tracking are far from perfect. Filters generally block too much—and too little. And surfers can block IP-address tracking by using services such as Zero Knowledge's Freedom or anonymizer.com. In any case, knowing where a user is is only part of the solution. In the case of Yahoo!, the firm would still have to work out which auctions to block.

But do these shortcomings matter? Jack Goldsmith, a law professor at the University of Chicago, argues that the real world is full of imperfect filtering and identification techniques: criminals crack safes, 15-year-olds visit bars with fake IDs, secret information is leaked to the press. To Mr Goldsmith, there is little doubt that filtering and identification technologies will help to make cyberspace more regulated, because they will allow governments to raise the cost of getting certain information.

China, for instance, has essentially covered its territory with an Intranet isolated from the rest of the online world by software that blocks access to sites with unwanted content. Although clever surfers can find ways to tunnel through the "Great Firewall", it keeps the majority from straying too far online. Most Chinese, in any case, get on to the Internet from work or a public place, where the state can control the software and track what users do, and where they risk being seen if they go to an illegal site.

These technologies are likely to become more efficient. The demands of e-commerce, rather than governments, are driving improvements. Akamai, an Internet firm which speeds up delivery by using a network of computers to store online content closer to consumers, recently started offering a new service called EdgeScape. This allows websites to determine exactly where a visitor is, at the time he visits, in order to customise content by region or country.

Online companies will certainly also make use in the future of a controversial feature called IP v6, designed by the Internet Engineering Task Force (IETF). At present, the anonymity of most Internet users is more or less protected because service providers generally assign a different IP address each time someone logs on. But IP v6 includes a new, expanded IP address, part of which is the unique serial number of each computer's network-connection hardware. Every data packet sent will carry a user's electronic fingerprints.

The holy grail for e-commerce, however, would be a system in which users had permanent digital certificates on their computers containing details of age, citizenship, sex, professional credentials, and so on. Such technology would not only allow websites to aim their services at individuals, but would let governments reclaim their authority. These solutions to Internet regulation are far off, if they fly at all. But Lawrence Lessig, a law professor at Stanford University, warns that e-commerce firms will push for such certificates and that governments may one day require them.

Nor do governments always need new technology to impose their regulatory muscle. They can also rely on human intervention, just as Yahoo! now intends to do in order to ban auctions of Nazi and Ku Klux Klan items on its site. Although it is coy about details, the company says it will use software to filter out objectionable material and human reviewers to decide borderline cases.

Indirect regulation can also do the job. In Myanmar, formerly Burma, access to the web is banned. To enforce this, the country's military regime imposes jail terms of up to 15 years for unauthorised use of a modem. China recently published sweeping new rules that require Internet companies to apply for a licence and hold them responsible for illegal content carried on their websites. And democratic governments are learning that illegal commercial activity, such as online gambling, can be regulated by controlling credit-card companies and other financial intermediaries.

Multinational Efforts

Perhaps the most promising approach, from the governments' point of view, is co-ordinated action to gain some control over the online world. Faster than might be expected, countries have banded together to fight the threat of jurisdictional arbitrage and to solve conflicts of law. The most straightforward way for governments to do that is to devise a uniform international standard. One early example is the World Intellectual Property Organisation's copyright treaty of 1996, which strengthened international copyright rules.

> *"China recently published sweeping new rules that . . . hold [Internet companies] responsible for illegal content carried on their websites."*

The Council of Europe—a group of 41 countries which includes all 15 members of the European Union—is putting the finishing touches to the world's first international treaty on cybercrime. The United States, which has also been involved in the negotiations, supports the treaty's main points. Signatories to the agreement, which will probably be presented for ratification this summer, must have laws on their books that allow, for instance, quick seizure of incriminating computer data and its distribution to authorities in other countries.

Such harmonisation is most likely in areas of interest to big multinational corporations (copyright) or where the interests of countries are closely aligned (crime and taxation). On January 9th, the OECD [Organisation for Economic Co-Operation and Development] countries announced that they had agreed on a series of rules determining what kind of e-commerce activities made a company liable to taxation: doing business through a website, they concluded, would not leave a company liable to tax in the country from which the website had been accessed.

> *"The Department of Commerce and e-commerce firms are pushing for ... a new system of private laws."*

But even most democratic countries are unlikely to agree on standards for more controversial issues, above all freedom of speech. As a result, in many areas, governments are trying "softer" approaches.

Different Approaches to Privacy Protection

In the case of privacy, for instance, the United States and the EU have agreed to disagree. America so far favours self-regulation and sectoral laws, for example for the health-care industry, in order to protect the personal data of its citizens. In contrast, the EU relies on comprehensive privacy legislation enforced by data-protection agencies. The EU's privacy directive also authorises member states to cut off the data flow to other countries, including the United States, which do not have (by its lights) adequate privacy laws.

To avoid a trade war over personal data, both sides devised a "safe-harbour" agreement that went into effect on November 1st. This protects companies from having their data flow severed, as long as their privacy policies comply with certain principles (such as letting consumers choose how data are used, and allowing access to that data). So far, however, only a dozen companies and organisations have registered with America's Department of Commerce, not least because many firms first want to see whether and how the agreement will be enforced.

The provisions of the Hague Convention could prove more popular. This treaty, which is due to be adopted at a diplomatic conference in June, was first proposed by the American government in the early 1990s to formalise worldwide what American courts already often do: enforce foreign judgments in matters such as intellectual-property claims, contractual disputes and libel. American citizens would thus also be able to collect awards abroad.

Under the treaty, an online store could be liable under laws in any of the 48 member-countries of the Hague conference. That is why the American government is opposing, among other things, a clause that would ensure that consumers could sue businesses in the courts of the country where the consumer lives.

Instead, the Department of Commerce and e-commerce firms are pushing for a different solution: in effect, a new system of private laws, which would avoid the requirement to abide by the laws of the countries where their customers live. As in the Safe Harbour agreement, web firms could seek a certification that they follow certain minimum rules of consumer protection and privacy. Conflicts would be resolved by so-called "alternative dispute resolution".

Will these trends turn cyberspace into a place stuffed with even more rules than the real world, as online companies worry? Or, as free-speech advocates predict, will litigants and governments pursue service providers they don't like, leading to an ever-tighter standard for protected speech?

A Critical Juncture

For now, these fears seem exaggerated. But much depends on how the legal and political battles of the next few years are settled, and how technology evolves. There have been some attempts to steer a middle course. The Brussels Convention, for instance, lets consumers sue a foreign website in their home country only if the site can be proved to have aimed at that country's market.

Many courts are likely to refuse to enforce foreign judgments on matters of widely differing practice, especially where free speech is concerned. For example, Yahoo! will probably successfully defend itself in the American courts, on first amendment grounds, against the French judgment.

And yet this may not be enough. The company plans to go on fighting the legal case. On December 22nd [2000] it asked a federal court for a ruling stating that a French court cannot hold an American-based company accountable for breaking French law. Nevertheless, the company has already, in effect, caved in by banning Nazi memorabilia from its auction sites. So whatever the American courts decide, the outcome will be new restrictions on Yahoo!'s American operations.

The firms that will be easiest to regulate and restrict, and which will be subject to multiple jurisdictions, will be those with assets in several

> *"Peer-to-peer networks could make it more difficult to control content on the Internet."*

countries: big websites such as Yahoo!, Amazon and eBay. But this is nothing new, Mr Goldsmith argues: multinational companies have always faced multiple regulatory burdens. In addition, new technology will make it much easier to comply. Several start-ups such as Mercury2, MyCustoms.com and tariffic.com already offer services that automate the process of making sure that cross-border trade complies with all the various rules.

For Michael Froomkin, a law professor at the University of Miami, all this represents a great irony about the Internet. What was supposed to be an anarchistic and liberating technology may in fact make the world less democratic, by forcing a huge increase in legal harmonisation. This will mostly be pursued by governments and vested interests banding together to enact multilateral treaties, which are difficult for national parliaments to scrutinise or change.

The Hague convention and the cybercrime treaty are cases in point. If the online industry creates its own way of resolving disputes, this could take away jurisdiction from courts worldwide and eliminate existing legal rights. And the fact that the American government let a relatively unknown European organisation develop such an important agreement as the cybercrime treaty is a sign that Washington did not want it widely discussed. Although negotiations began three years ago, the treaty was made public only last April, in its 22nd draft. Only recently, therefore, were Internet advocacy groups able to get involved. To them, the treaty is a document that "threatens the rights of the individual while extending the power of police authorities."

The treaty also exemplifies the risk that governments, especially democratic ones, run when they try to assert their authority in the online world. The legal tools and technologies they develop, though useful in that context, may well be abused not only by them but also by authoritarian governments. The means used by France to fight anti-Semitism on the web could also be used to prevent people living in less democratic countries from getting the information they need to strive for basic freedoms.

Freedom Still Thrives on the Internet

Those aiming to preserve the Internet's freedom-loving character also have new technologies to deploy in their battle with government regulators. So-called peer-to-peer networks could make it more difficult to control content on the Internet. FreeNet, for instance, automatically spreads copies of documents all over the web, so that they no longer belong to one place. And SafeWeb will soon launch a service called "Triangle Boy" that allows netizens in democratic countries to turn their PCs into so-called proxy servers. These can then be used by surfers in China, Saudi Arabia or Vietnam to pierce through their countries' firewalls.

On the Internet, the struggle between freedom and state control will rage for some time. But if recent trends in online regulation prove anything, it is that technology is being used by both sides in this battle and that freedom is by no means certain to win. The Internet could indeed become the most liberating technology since the printing press—but only if governments let it.

Government Regulation of the Internet Is Necessary

by Debora Spar

About the author: *Debora Spar is a professor at the Harvard Business School and the author of* Pirates, Prophets, and Pioneers: Business and Politics Along the Technological Frontier.

A long, long time ago—in about, say, March 1999—a crop of scruffy prophets trumpeted the coming of a new economy. Waving IPOs (initial public offerings) and visions of vast riches, these New Age gurus declared that technology would solve all mankind's ills and that the market had at last triumphed over all that might restrain it. Societies were now free from meddlesome authorities, they declared, and governments were all but dead.

In the new economy, it appeared, individuals—the great, the good, the weak and the small—would be free at last from the bonds that had historically tied them. They would be free to write subversive prose and avoid national boundaries and launch dotcom boutiques. There weren't supposed to be any big players in this virgin techno-land: the miracles of the internet would flatten old hierarchies to their thinnest plank. No longer tied to the corporate beast, the new woman in the grey flannel two-piece suit would leap from her cubicle, proclaim a revolution and be instantly bombarded by hordes of angel investors.

Yet today, the new economy seems reeling. Even before terrorists smashed into the heart of New York [during the September 11 terrorist attacks], the start-up boom in both the United States and Europe had already busted, and plummeting technology stocks cast an ever-widening shadow across the financial markets that spawned them. Are we witnessing the death of what should have been our future?

A Predictable Cycle

Not really. It's all just part of a fairly predictable cycle, one that accompanies most technological breakthroughs, and should have been apparent from the start. Consider what happened in 1896, when a young inventor named Guglielmo Marconi first brought his "wireless telegraph" to Britain. Nervous customs officials seized the box, claiming that it could only be used for subversion, and bureaucrats of the postal system scoffed. Later, when the magic of Marconi's radio was made apparent, average citizens flocked to hear his ethereal broadcasts and feted the inventor as a king. As radio use became more widespread, awestruck listeners claimed that it was truly a revolutionary technology—something that could never be regulated or controlled. Indeed, in the US, where radio remained unregulated for decades, investors poured into radio stocks, helping to drive the market frenzy of the 1920s.

Sound familiar? It should. What happened in the radio industry is remarkably similar to what is happening today. Then, as now, a series of technological advances led to the creation of a market space, mesmerising in terms of both its commercial and societal impact. With radio, citizens were suddenly able to pull information down from the "ether", catching whispers and music from far-off signals. People could communicate across thin air, going around governments that had long endeavoured to control communications, and launching the phenomenon of broadcasting.

> *"What happened in the radio industry is remarkably similar to what is happening [to the Internet] today."*

From today's perspective, what is most interesting about the radio story is how quickly the technology was reined in. In the United Kingdom, for example, the government swiftly brought Marconi's empire more under its own control. It imposed significant constraints on radio traffic in 1906, purchased all of the Marconi Company's coastal stations in 1909, and then drew the whole industry to its side during the First World War. After the war, when a new round of innovators figured out how to transmit voice and music along the radio waves (Marconi had transmitted only the beeps of Morse code), the government established the BBC as Britain's radio monopoly.

In the US, government involvement was slower but no less definitive. In the aftermath of war, the US navy brought all of radio's key patents under its control and then bundled them into the newly created Radio Corporation of America. It then moved—reluctantly but forcefully—into the regulatory sphere, parsing the radio spectrum into distinct segments and allocating them to specific firms. By the 1930s, radio in both the US and Britain was a heavily concentrated, tightly regulated industry.

We see a similar cycle in the early days of the telegraph, and in the more recent evolution of satellite television. In these industries, too, an early wave of enthusiasm gave rise to dreams of anarchy. Entrepreneurs built huge empires—John Pender's Cable & Wireless, Murdoch's BSkyB—on the back of technological innovation, and were able either to circumvent government authority or to tie it to their needs.

In far-flung places such as India or China, the new technology was seen as a distinctly political tool: a way to extend imperial power in India, a means of circumventing the government in China. And for a while, and to some extent, it worked. But ultimately, the same fate that befell radio hit telegraphs and satellites: governments moved in, the rules fell in place, and the markets returned to normalcy.

As the Euphoria Wears Off

Today, the so-called new economy is experiencing the latest round of this cycle. In the heady days of the internet boom, there was a general sense that governments were dead and that markets had killed them. Newborn companies were giddy with the freedom that money had bestowed upon them and the architecture of the net seemed technically immune to control.

This euphoria lasted for roughly five years, from the IPO boom of the mid-1990s to the Nasdaq tumble that began in 2000. It is critical to note, however, that the up-and-down cycle of the new economy is not just about share prices and start-up firms. It is not just about entrepreneurs creating a buzz that ultimately proved unfounded. Rather, what is unfolding here is a fundamental readjustment of rules and power, the same kind of readjustment that occurred in earlier industries.

What is driving this readjustment has less to do with markets or money than with the fundamental demand for order. In the early days of the internet, as in any rush for wealth, people were relatively content to live with anarchy. They were willing to risk their privacy in order to list their book preferences on amazon.com. They were willing to sacrifice property rights to the joys of downloading songs from napster.com. But once the thrill of the new had started to subside, people became more cognisant of the costs that came riding alongside the net. They realised suddenly that property rights and privacy were not to be blithely discarded. They grew wary of the terrorist in the chatroom, tired of the junk mail that masqueraded as news. And thus they began to push for rules.

Developments in the financial markets accentuated these trends. Once the Nasdaq began its perilous decline, investors started to tremble anew at the emperor's potential nakedness. They began demanding more rigorous accounting practices and increased oversight of what were once market darlings. This caution set off the pessimism that dogs us today.

> *"Governments will impose their laws upon the internet."*

If we look at the current situation from a historical perspective, the next rounds of evolution are relatively clear. The internet economy certainly isn't going away, and the technologies that lie at its base will continue to affect the way we work, play and organise our societies.

In countries such as China and Saudi Arabia, where governments have historically tried to control the flow of information among their citizens, the net could well prove revolutionary, creating new places for dissidence to thrive. Elsewhere, however, the new economy seems destined to follow along the course laid out by the old.

Having passed through the initial wave of innovation and enthusiasm, markets that cluster around the information industries will begin to settle into middle age. Some firms will get fatter and more complacent. Most will not make it. Governments will impose their laws upon the internet. This will prove tricky, because the net is still a slippery medium and crosses borders imperceptibly. But governments will nevertheless enforce rules in cyberspace that their citizens are likely to obey.

This is not the vision that roused the spirits of the net's first pioneers. Governments were not supposed to trample into this new-found space or disturb the liberty that survived there. The problem with too much liberty, though, is that it turns rapidly into anarchy. And anarchy is simply not conducive to commerce. The task facing government is to step back into this once new economy and establish the rules that will allow it to prosper.

Stronger Internet Privacy Laws Are Necessary

by Simson Garfinkel

About the author: *Simson Garfinkel is a columnist for the* Boston Globe *and the author of* Database Nation: The Death of Privacy in the 21st Century.

You wake to the sound of a ringing telephone—but how could that happen? Several months ago, you reprogrammed your home telephone system so it would never ring before the civilized hour of 8 A.M. But it's barely 6:45. Who was able to bypass your phone's programming?

You pick up the receiver, then slam it down a moment later. It's one of those marketing machines playing a recorded message. What's troubling you now is how this call got past the filters you set up. Later on you'll discover how: The company that sold you the phone created an undocumented "back door"; last week, the phone codes were sold in an online auction.

Now that you're awake, you decide to go through yesterday's mail. There's a letter from the neighborhood hospital you visited last month. "We're pleased that our emergency room could serve you in your time of need," the letter begins. "As you know, our fees (based on our agreement with your HMO) do not cover the cost of treatment. To make up the difference, a number of hospitals have started selling patient records to medical researchers and consumer-marketing firms. Rather than mimic this distasteful behavior, we have decided to ask you to help us make up the difference. We are recommending a tax-deductible contribution of $275 to help defray the cost of your visit."

The veiled threat isn't empty, but you decide you don't really care who finds out about your sprained wrist. You fold the letter in half and drop it into your shredder. Also into the shredder goes a trio of low-interest credit-card offers. Why a shredder? A few years ago you would never have thought of shredding your junk mail—until a friend in your apartment complex had his identity "stolen" by the building's superintendent. As best as anybody can figure out, the super picked one of those preapproved credit-card applications out of the trash, called the toll-free number and picked up the card when it was delivered. He's in Mexico now, with a lot of expensive clothing and electronics, all at your friend's expense.

On that cheery note, you grab your bag and head out the door, which automatically locks behind you.

This is the future—not a far-off future but one that's just around the corner. It's a future in which what little privacy we now have will be gone. Some people call this loss of privacy "Orwellian," harking back to *1984*, George Orwell's classic work on privacy and autonomy. In that book, Orwell imagined a future in which a totalitarian state used spies, video surveillance, historical revisionism and control over the media to maintain its power. But the age of monolithic state control is over. The future we're rushing toward isn't one in which our every move is watched and recorded by some all-knowing Big Brother. It is instead a future of a hundred kid brothers who constantly watch and interrupt our daily lives. Orwell thought the Communist system represented the ultimate threat to individual liberty. Over the next fifty years, we will see new kinds of threats to privacy that find their roots not in Communism but in capitalism, the free market, advanced technology and the unbridled exchange of electronic information.

The problem with this word "privacy" is that it falls short of conveying the really big picture. Privacy isn't just about hiding things. It's about self-possession, autonomy and integrity. As we move into the computerized world of the twenty-first century, privacy will be one of our

> *"Over the next 50 years, we will see new kinds of threats to privacy that find their roots not in Communism, but in capitalism."*

most important civil rights. But this right of privacy isn't the right of people to close their doors and pull down their window shades—perhaps because they want to engage in some sort of illicit or illegal activity. It's the right of people to control what details about their lives stay inside their own houses and what leaks to the outside.

Most of us recognize that our privacy is at risk. According to a 1996 nationwide poll conducted by Louis Harris & Associates, 24 percent of Americans have "personally experienced a privacy invasion." In 1995 the same survey found that 80 percent felt that "consumers have lost all control over how personal information about them is circulated and used by companies." Ironically, both the 1995 and 1996 surveys were paid for by Equifax, a company that earns nearly $2 billion each year from collecting and distributing personal information.

Technology and Privacy Invasion

Today the Internet is compounding our privacy conundrum—largely because the voluntary approach to privacy protection advocated by the Clinton Administration doesn't work in the rough and tumble world of real business. For example, a study released by the California HealthCare Foundation found that nineteen of the top twenty-one health websites have privacy policies, but most sites fail to follow them. Not surprisingly, 17 percent of Americans questioned in a poll said they do not go online for health information because of privacy concerns.

But privacy threats are not limited to the Internet: Data from all walks of life are now being captured, compiled, indexed and stored. For example, New York City has now deployed the Metrocard system, which allows subway and bus riders to pay their fares by simply swiping a magnetic-strip card. But the system also records the serial number of each card and the time and location of every swipe. New York police have used this vast database to crack crimes and disprove alibis. Although law enforcement is a reasonable use of this database, it is also a use that was adopted without any significant public debate. Furthermore, additional controls may be necessary: It is not clear who has access to the database, under what circumstances that access is given and what provisions are being taken to prevent the introduction of false data into it. It would be terrible if the subway's database were used by an employee to stalk an ex-lover or frame an innocent person for a heinous crime.

"New technology has brought extraordinary benefits to society, but it also has placed all of us in an electronic fishbowl in which our habits, tastes and activities are watched and recorded," New York State Attorney General Eliot Spitzer said in late January [2001], in announcing that Chase Manhattan had agreed to stop selling depositor information without clear permission from customers. "Personal information thought to be confidential is routinely shared with others without our consent."

Loss of Privacy Is Not Inevitable

Today's war on privacy is intimately related to the recent dramatic advances in technology. Many people today say that in order to enjoy the benefits of modern society, we must necessarily relinquish some degree of privacy. If we want the convenience of paying for a meal by credit card or paying for a toll with an electronic tag mounted on our rearview mirror, then we must accept the routine collection of our purchases and driving habits in a large database over which we have no control. It's a simple bargain, albeit a Faustian one.

This trade-off is both unnecessary and wrong. It reminds me of another crisis our society faced back in the fifties and sixties—the environmental crisis. Then, advocates of big business said that poisoned rivers and lakes were the necessary costs of economic development, jobs and an improved standard of living. Poison was progress: Anybody who argued otherwise simply didn't understand the facts.

Today we know better. Today we know that sustainable economic development depends on preserving the environment. Indeed, preserving the environment is a prerequisite to the survival of the human race. Without clean air to breathe and clean water to drink, we will all die. Similarly, in order to reap the benefits of technology, it is more important than ever for us to use technology to protect personal freedom. . . .

Privacy-invasive technology does not exist in a vacuum, of course. That's because technology itself exists at a junction between science, the market and society. People create technology to fill specific needs and desires. And technology is regulated, or not, as people and society see fit. Few engineers set out to build systems designed to crush privacy and autonomy, and few businesses or consumers would willingly use or purchase these systems if they understood the consequences.

How can we keep technology and the free market from killing our privacy? One way is by being careful and informed consumers. Some people have begun taking simple measures to protect their privacy, measures like making purchases with cash and refusing to provide their Social Security numbers—or providing fake ones. And a small but growing number of people are speaking out for technology with privacy. In 1990 Lotus and Equifax teamed up to create a CD-ROM product called "Lotus Marketplace: Households," which would have included names, addresses and demographic information on every household in the United States, so small businesses could do the same kind of target marketing that big businesses have been doing since the sixties. The project was canceled when more than 30,000 people wrote to Lotus demanding that their names be taken out of the database. . . .

Federal Privacy-Protection Efforts

But individual actions are not enough. We need to involve government itself in the privacy fight. The biggest privacy failure of the US government has been its failure to carry through with the impressive privacy groundwork that was laid in the Nixon, Ford and Carter administrations. It's worth taking a look back at that groundwork and considering how it may serve us today.

The seventies were a good decade for privacy protection and consumer rights. In 1970 Congress passed the Fair Credit Reporting Act, which gave Americans the previously denied right to see their own credit reports and demand the removal of erroneous information. Elliot Richardson, who at the time was President Nixon's Secretary of Health, Education and Welfare, created a commission in 1972 to study the impact of computers on privacy. After years of testimony in Congress, the commission found all the more reason for alarm and issued a landmark report in 1973.

> *"We need to involve government itself in the privacy fight."*

The most important contribution of the Richardson report was a bill of rights for the computer age, which it called the Code of Fair Information Practices. The code is based on five principles:

- There must be no personal-data record-keeping system whose very existence is secret.
- There must be a way for a person to find out what information about the person is in a record and how it is used.
- There must be a way for a person to prevent information about the person that was obtained for one purpose from being used or made available for other purposes without the person's consent.
- There must be a way for a person to correct or amend a record of identifiable information about the person.
- Any organization creating, maintaining, using or disseminating records of identifiable personal data must assure the reliability of the data for their intended use and must take precautions to prevent misuse of the data.

The biggest impact of the Richardson report wasn't in the United States but in Europe. In the years after the report was published, practically every European country passed laws based on these principles. Many created data-protection commissions and commissioners to enforce the laws. Some believe that one reason for Europe's interest in electronic privacy was its experience with Nazi Germany in the thirties and forties. Hitler's secret police used the records of governments and private organizations in the countries he invaded to round up people who posed the greatest threat to German occupation; postwar Europe realized the danger of allowing potentially threatening private information to be collected, even by democratic governments that might be responsive to public opinion.

> *"Both the Bush and Clinton administrations waged an all-out war against the rights of computer users to engage in private and secure communications."*

But here in the United States, the idea of institutionalized data protection faltered. President Jimmy Carter showed interest in improving medical privacy, but he was quickly overtaken by economic and political events. Carter lost the election of 1980 to Ronald Reagan, whose aides saw privacy protection as yet another failed Carter initiative. Although several privacy-protection laws were signed during the Reagan/Bush era, the leadership for these bills came from Congress, not the White House. The lack of leadership stifled any chance of passing a nationwide data-protection act. Such an act would give people the right to know if their name and personal information is stored in a database, to see the information and to demand that incorrect information be removed.

An Alarming Trend

In fact, while most people in the federal government were ignoring the cause of privacy, some were actually pursuing an antiprivacy agenda. In the early eighties, the government initiated numerous "computer matching" programs designed to catch fraud and abuse. Unfortunately, because of erroneous data these programs often penalized innocent people. In 1994 Congress passed the Communications Assistance to Law Enforcement Act, which gave the government dramatic new powers for wiretapping digital communications. In 1996 Congress passed two laws, one requiring states to display Social Security numbers on driver's licenses and another requiring that all medical patients in the United States be issued unique numerical identifiers, even if they pay their own bills. Fortunately, the implementation of those 1996 laws has been delayed, thanks largely to a citizen backlash and the resulting inaction by Congress and the executive branch.

> *"The Fair Credit Reporting Act was a good law in its day, but it should be upgraded into a Data Protection Act."*

Continuing the assault, both the Bush and Clinton administrations waged an all-out war against the rights of computer users to engage in private and secure communications. Starting in 1991, both administrations floated proposals for use of "Clipper" encryption systems that would have given the government access to encrypted personal communications. Only recently did the Clinton Administration finally relent in its seven-year war against computer privacy. President Clinton also backed the Communications Decency Act (CDA), which made it a crime to transmit sexually explicit information to minors—and, as a result, might have required Internet providers to deploy far-reaching monitoring and censorship systems. When a court in Philadelphia found the CDA unconstitutional, the Clinton Administration appealed the decision all the way to the Supreme Court—and lost.

One important step toward reversing the current direction of government would be to create a permanent federal oversight agency charged with protecting privacy. Such an agency would:

- Watch over the government's tendency to sacrifice people's privacy for other goals and perform governmentwide reviews of new federal programs for privacy violations before they're launched.
- Enforce the government's few existing privacy laws.
- Be a guardian for individual privacy and liberty in the business world, showing businesses how they can protect privacy and profits at the same time.
- Be an ombudsman for the American public and rein in the worst excesses that our society has created.

Evan Hendricks, editor of the Washington-based newsletter *Privacy Times,* estimates that a fifty-person privacy-protection agency could be created with an annual budget of less than $5 million—a tiny drop in the federal budget.

Some privacy activists scoff at the idea of using government to assure our privacy. Governments, they say, are responsible for some of the greatest privacy violations of all time. This is true, but the US government was also one of the greatest polluters of all time. Today the government is the nation's environmental police force, equally scrutinizing the actions of private business and the government itself. . . .

A National Data Protection Act

The Fair Credit Reporting Act was a good law in its day, but it should be upgraded into a Data Protection Act. Unfortunately, the Federal Trade Commission and the courts have narrowly interpreted the FCRA. The first thing that is needed is legislation that expands it into new areas. Specifically, consumer-reporting firms should be barred from reporting arrests unless those arrests result in convictions. Likewise, consumer-reporting firms should not be allowed to report evictions unless they result in court judgments in favor of the landlord or a settlement in which both the landlord and tenant agree that the eviction can be reported. Companies should be barred from exchanging medical information about individuals or furnishing medical information as part of a patient's report without the patient's explicit consent.

> *"Today, technology is killing one of our most cherished freedoms."*

We also need new legislation that expands the fundamental rights offered to consumers under the FCRA. When negative information is reported to a credit bureau, the business making that report should be required to notify the subject of the report—the consumer—in writing. Laws should be clarified so that if a consumer-reporting company does not correct erroneous data in its reports, consumers can sue for real damages, punitive damages and legal fees. People should have the right to correct any false information in their files, and if the consumer and the business disagree about the truth, then the consumer should have a right to place a detailed explanation into his or her record. And people should have a right to see all the information that has been collected on them; these reports should be furnished for free, at least once every six months.

We need to rethink consent, a bedrock of modern law. Consent is a great idea, but the laws that govern consent need to be rewritten to limit what kinds of agreements can be made with consumers. Blanket, perpetual consent should be outlawed.

Further, we need laws that require improved computer security. In the eighties the United States aggressively deployed cellular-telephone and alphanumeric-pager networks, even though both systems were fundamentally unsecure. Instead of deploying secure systems, manufacturers lobbied for laws that would make it illegal to listen to the broadcasts. The results were predictable: dozens of cases in which radio transmissions were eavesdropped. We are now making similar mistakes in the prosecution of many Internet crimes, going after the perpetrator while refusing to acknowledge the liabilities of businesses that do not even take the most basic security precautions.

We should also bring back the Office of Technology Assessment, set up under a bill passed in 1972. The OTA didn't have the power to make laws or issue regulations, but it could publish reports on topics Congress asked it to study. Among other things, the OTA considered at length the trade-offs between law enforcement and civil liberties, and it also looked closely at issues of worker monitoring. In total, the OTA published 741 reports, 175 of which dealt directly with privacy issues, before it was killed in 1995 by the newly elected Republican-majority Congress.

The Right to Digital Self-Determination

Nearly forty years ago, Rachel Carson's book *Silent Spring* helped seed the US environmental movement. And to our credit, the silent spring that Carson foretold never came to be. *Silent Spring* was successful because it helped people to understand the insidious damage that pesticides were wreaking on the environment, and it helped our society and our planet to plot a course to a better future.

Today, technology is killing one of our most cherished freedoms. Whether you call this freedom the right to digital self-determination, the right to informational autonomy or simply the right to privacy, the shape of our future will be determined in large part by how we understand, and ultimately how we control or regulate, the threats to this freedom that we face today.

The Government Should Protect Children from Online Pornography

by Bruce Watson

About the author: *Bruce Watson is the president of Enough Is Enough, a nonprofit organization focused on making the Internet safer for children and families.*

How would you feel if your 11-year-old son went down to the public library and checked out *Deep Throat*, the hard-core pornographic video? Or your 9-year-old daughter stumbled across *Hustler* magazine during a research project in her classroom at school?

Most parents would experience something between shock and outrage, plus an element of pure surprise. But, of course, these are purely hypothetical examples—schools and libraries don't offer pornographic magazines and videos to kids. In fact, even for adults, it is almost unheard of for public libraries to have materials such as *Hustler* or *Deep Throat* in their print or video collections.

The Children's Internet Protection Act

So presumably the same standards also would apply on the Internet, right? The answer, unfortunately, is not yet, which is why Congress took a step in this direction in December [2000] by passing the Children's Internet Protection Act (CIPA). The CIPA offers a simple deal: if federal funds are used to provide Internet access in schools and libraries, then part of those funds must be used to filter out the pornography. (More precisely, child pornography, obscenity and material defined legally as "harmful to minors" must be filtered for minors age 16 or younger. For adult access, only the first two categories apply, with disabling available by a supervisor for research or other bona fide purposes.) Although CIPA was tucked into an appropriations bill, there is no question it was a response to widespread concern: A national survey last fall [2001] by Digital Media Forum found an overwhelming 92 percent support for filtering pornography out of school computers.

The reasons for concern have little to do with coyly posed *Playboy* center-folds. Even veteran pornographer Larry Flynt has acknowledged that "There's an awful lot of material on the Internet that children should not have access to. There's material that even I, in my wildest imagination, would not consider publishing." And much of it is freely available to anyone who stumbles onto a porn Website.

A study last summer for the National Center for Missing and Exploited Children found that one in four online youths ages 10 to 17 had an unwanted encounter with pornography in the previous 12 months. Children today are encountering these hard-core sites through misleading site names (such as whitehouse.com, a porn site), through invisible "metatags" misusing popular brand names such as Nintendo or Muppets, through unsolicited e-mail or simply by typing the word "porn" into an unfiltered Internet browser. Curiosity in children and teenagers is natural and healthy, but the distorted lens of hard-core porn offers a poor sexual role model.

> *"Even veteran pornographer Larry Flynt has acknowledged that 'There's an awful lot of material on the Internet that children should not have access to.'"*

So why is CIPA vehemently opposed by groups such as the American Civil Liberties Union (ACLU) and their friends at the American Library Association (ALA)? Their public posture is that CIPA might be well-intended, but technical difficulties make all such legislation unworkable. Closer inspection reveals that the real debate is philosophical.

The Overblown Problem of Overblocking

Opponents of filtering say the software has too many anomalies, such as "overblocking" Websites for chicken-breast recipes or the county of Middlesex. Such examples often are based on first-generation word-association software rather than state-of-the-art products. They reflect the astonishingly persistent disinformation campaign waged by filtering opponents. Other examples, rather than confirming a sinister political agenda, have an almost hilariously random quality, such as the famous (and brief) blocking by one product of the Quaker church Website.

The real question is not whether filters are perfect—if you use Windows, you know that perfection is an impossible standard in the world of computers and, thus, irrelevant. The real question is whether they work within a tolerable level of error. Experience in schools and libraries indicates that the good brands meet this test comfortably. The performance of the better products is one reason why the number of libraries using filters has doubled in the last two years. Approximately 25 percent of libraries now use at least some filtering, according to the National Commission on Library Science.

Besides, how can today's filtering software be described as a one-size-fits-all solution when the industrial-strength products for schools and libraries typically have between 20 and 60 categories of customization available? Do the math—that's a dizzying range of permutations.

The ACLU/ALA strategy is fairly straightforward: By relentlessly publicizing the "anomaly of the week," they distract attention from the inherent absurdity of their own demand—that only a perfect filter is acceptable in the imperfect world of computers. They would have us believe that a single overblocked site is a more significant anomaly than an entire generation of schoolchildren given free and easy access to the crudest of hard-core pornography. It's easy to see why 92 percent of the public disagrees with them.

The ALAs solution is to promote "acceptable-use policies" in each local library. The only problem is they don't work. More than 90 percent of public libraries already have such policies, yet former librarian David Burt's study, *Dangerous Access* (2000 Edition), found thousands of incidents of library patrons accessing pornography online. The more disturbing incidents included public masturbation, adults enticing children to view porn sites and trading in child pornography. Burt filed requests under the Freedom of Information Act for incident reports concerning Internet pornography but received only a 29 percent response rate after the ALA got involved. So much for open access to information.

The ACLU and ALA argue that CIPA is too vague because just about anything might be considered "harmful to minors" by someone. However, this legally defined term already is used in the print world, and there is scant evidence of "rogue" prosecutions. The courts have made clear that this term cannot be extended to mere nudity or sexual information, regardless of how controversial the political or sexual viewpoints may be. The harsh reality is that commercial porn sites now display a host of free materials that are harmful to minors or even obscene under almost any standard. The Pink Kitty Porn Palace Website isn't showing AIDS-prevention information or video tours of the Louvre.

> *"If schools and libraries provide unfiltered access [to the Internet], then public funds are being used to distribute pornography."*

The Issue of Censorship

A more serious concern, especially for conservatives, is whether it is necessary for the government to step in and require filtering. Part of the answer is that, if schools and libraries provide unfiltered access only, then public funds are being used to distribute pornography. When government funds are creating the problem, government funds should provide the solution. Requiring the feds to clean up their own mess is hardly a "big-government" proposition.

The other reason for a legislated approach is that the group that could help most—the ALA—is instead leading the opposition. Says Judith Krug, director of the ALA's Office of Intellectual Freedom: "Blocking material leads to censorship. That goes for pornography and bestiality, too. If you don't like it, don't look at it." This applies even for children. Their fetchingly titled manual, *The Censor Is Coming—Intellectual Freedom for Children*, notes that, by formal policy, "the ALA opposes all attempts to restrict access to library services, materials and facilities based on the age of library users." The fierce opposition of ALA's Head Office is the principal reason why 75 percent of libraries use no filtering today.

When communities fret that this ivory-tower approach makes local libraries unsafe for children, Krug responds: "If you don't want your children to access that information, you had better be with your children when they use a computer." Former ALA president Ann Symons explains: "We do not help children when we simply wall them off from information and ideas that are controversial and disturbing." The fallacy, of course, is to equate pornography with information and ideas. Hard-core pornography is simply not an intellectual matter; rather, like the Bill Clinton/Monica Lewinsky affair, the guiding impulse for porn comes from another part of the anatomy.

Another ALA mantra is that government can't censor and, because libraries are government-funded, therefore libraries can't censor. This catchy sound bite is meaningless. Government funds also are used for office buildings, theaters and public parks—each with quite different First Amendment protection. The mantra also ignores the critical difference between the government as sovereign (the king can't restrict his subjects' private speech) and the government as patron (the king does not have to support every artistic or literary endeavor).

The Hypocrisy of the ALA

The selective way the ALA applies its own dogma is even more intriguing. Last summer a Toledo, Ohio, couple contributed a critical biography of Planned Parenthood founder Margaret Sanger to their local library because none of the library's 20-odd books on the subject mentioned her controversial views on race or eugenics. The library declined the gift because "the author's political and social agenda . . . is not appropriate." Contacted by *WorldNetDaily* for comment, the ALA's Krug—oblivious to the irony—blandly explained that librarians can determine "what materials are useful for their community." This is the same official whose response to community concerns about Internet porn is, "If you don't like it, don't look at it."

Under the ALA's definition of intellectual freedom, it apparently is just fine for government employees (librarians) to exclude materials from a public library because of "the author's political and social agenda," but it would be censorship for private citizens to question the wisdom of providing hard-core pornography. Perchance the ALA has a "political and social agenda" of its own?

Inevitably, CIPA will spend the next few years tied up in legal challenges by the ACLU (and possibly the ALA). The ACLU still trumpets its low-grade win in a Virginia District Court against the Loudon County library. The judge compared filtering to ripping pages out of an encyclopedia, forgetting that any encyclopedia is but a single published work, while the Internet is an entire medium, like TV. (Libraries that provide PBS programming feel no obligation to add the Spice Channel.) For various reasons, the independent *TechLaw Journal* concluded, "The library would probably win before the 4th Circuit Court of Appeals, if it were to appeal."

The library's decision not to appeal was colored by the magnitude of the plaintiff's legal fees if it lost. Even at the district-court level, the fees presented by the ACLU and coplaintiffs People for the American Way were a speech-chilling $488,601, compared to the $55,000 paid to the library's attorneys. Fortunately, such intimidation will have less weight against the CIPA, where the defendant will be the Bush Department of Justice.

In conclusion, it is important to remember that parents still have the primary responsibility for guiding their children on the Internet, just as they do on issues like smoking or drinking. The problem is that parents today carry all the responsibility, even though they usually are less computer-literate than their children. Parents need the support of the law, just as they do with smoking and drinking. Children's safety online involves parents and other gatekeepers, the Internet industry and the legal community. It would be irresponsible for any of these groups to claim a free ride by having someone else shoulder the entire burden.

State Governments Should Be Able to Tax E-Commerce

by Frank Shafroth

About the author: *Frank Shafroth is director of state-federal relations for the National Governors Association, a lobbying organization that represents the nation's state governors.*

Currently, Internet-based merchants are not required to collect sales and use taxes, which places them at a significant advantage over traditional retailers. This inequity could have a profound negative impact on not only retailers but local communities because it risks states' ability to collect the revenue needed for education, police, and other essential services, and could lead to increases in state property or income taxes.

Nearly 40 percent of all state revenues come from the sales tax; it is the single most critical source of funding for public education in the United States. But, unless Congress moves to restore a level playing field, current industry and academic studies project states will lose between $10–20 billion in sales tax revenues by 2003.

The Internet Tax Freedom Act Harms State Economies

Many believe—incorrectly—that the Internet Tax Freedom Act (ITFA) passed by Congress in 1998 made the Internet tax-free. It did *not*. Businesses and consumers are charged taxes on Internet purchases from companies that have nexus in their state, and they are supposed to pay use taxes on the rest of their online purchases. The ITFA merely prevents states from adopting new Internet-specific taxes. But absent federal action, states may not require remote [out-of-state] sellers to collect the taxes owed on transactions. . . .

U.S. Supreme Court rulings prevent states from requiring sellers that do not have a physical presence in the state from collecting existing and legally owed

Excerpted from Frank Shafroth's testimony before the Senate Finance Committee on Tax Equity and Sovereignty for States in the Digital Age, August 1, 2001.

taxes on sales made into a state. With the advent of electronic commerce and the drastically increased ability to engage in remote marketing, the amount of uncollected revenue increases each year. Congress has steadfastly refused to grant states the authority to require remote sellers to collect these taxes, even though the Court has said it is squarely within their prerogative to do so.

The status quo means that remote sellers are not required to collect the state and local sales/use taxes except where they have a physical presence. The Mom and Pop retailer on Main Street or in the mall is required to charge, collect, and remit sales taxes to their respective governments. National retailers, which have a physical presence in most states, must collect

> *"The Internet Tax Freedom Act ... marks an extraordinary intrusion by Congress into one of the most fundamental aspects of [states' rights]."*

these taxes in their many stores, and through other ways (catalog, telephone, or Internet). Wal-Mart, Inc. files 10,000 different forms with various taxing jurisdictions across the country each year. E-tailers are exploiting this peculiar tax advantage in an industry with notoriously tight margins.

The Internet Tax Freedom Act applies only to state and local—not federal—taxes on the Internet. It marks an extraordinary intrusion by Congress into one of the most fundamental aspects of federalism: the responsibility and accountability of elected officials to the citizens who elected them. Some in Congress now may feel that micromanaging the state tax system has become part of its policy terrain. . . .

Electronic commerce has been an important component of the national economy since Marconi invented the telegraph and Alexander Graham Bell invented the telephone. Every credit card use involves the electronic transfer of data; the electronic transfer of accounts between banks is another form. No one has ever suggested that there was something so unique about these forms of electronic commerce that the federal government should prohibit the states from imposing taxes on transactions using these forms of electronic commerce.

Problems with the Current Law

Nevertheless, Congress enacted the Internet Tax Freedom Act (ITFA) in 1998. This legislation established a three-year moratorium on the state and local taxation of Internet access and "multiple or discriminatory taxes on electronic commerce." The ITFA provided "grandfather" protection for the states that were already applying these taxes on Internet access at the time of enactment. There were four aspects of this legislation that are troubling from the states' perspective:

• The first is that it preempted the states in determining whether Internet access should be subject to state taxation. The sales tax has been a mainstay of the state-local revenue structure for 65 years. For most of that period, Congress had the good sense to not mess with this revenue source. From a federalist perspective, the states should be making the decision about taxing Internet access.

• The second is that it has contributed to the myth that Internet transactions are tax-free. This, of course, is not true. Any seller with a presence in a state must collect the sales or use tax on transactions—in traditional stores, via mail-order, or from its website. Staples has a physical presence in 48 states, and it must collect the sales tax on purchases made by the residents of each of those states. Its affiliate, Staples.com, uses software to compute location-specific sales taxes. Only remote vendors that lack a physical presence in a state enjoy the advantages of not collecting the sales tax when residents of that state make remote purchases.

• Third is the troubling aspect of the vagueness of the definition of Internet access. With all the recent news about proposed purchases and mergers between cable and telecommunications firms, these developments raise the potential for the new firms to become dominant providers of Internet access. Would this be Internet access, cable, or telecommunications service? Would the service provide long distance phone calls, cable TV, movies on demand, and broadband Internet access? Governors believe that Internet content and services should not be exempted from state and local taxes. Governors believe it important for the committee to carefully evaluate the definition of access and maintain the current grandfather for the ten states that have continued their taxes. As we all know, the industry is moving to both bundle services such as television programs, games, books, music, and motion pictures into one fee, as well as to adapt rapidly changing technology.

> *"E-tailers are exploiting [their] peculiar tax advantage in an industry with notoriously tight margins."*

• The fourth, and most troubling, aspect of the ITFA is what appears to be exacerbating an increasing tendency of Congress to ignore its own house and intrude upon the responsibilities of states. There are multiple bills pending in the House and Senate today to interfere with existing state and local authority, regulations, and current revenues on Internet transactions. There are no comparable bills to limit federal taxes or authority. . . .

Establishing a Level Playing Field

Governors, state legislators, and other state organizations have worked hard on a compromise effort to break the stalemate on taxing retail electronic commerce. At the 2001 NGA Winter Meeting, policy EC-12, Streamlining State Sales Tax Systems, was reaffirmed. The policy calls for joint industry/government development of a simplified sales tax system, including streamlined administration and audit requirements, and uniform definitions of the goods and services that may be taxed. States retain the authority to determine what is taxed and at what rate. The policy establishes incentives for states to streamline and simplify their sales tax systems by calling on the federal government to restore fairness in the sales tax by requiring remote sellers to collect sales taxes for states that simplify their taxes. A minimum level of sales would be established; companies that made sales in the past year above that de minimus level would be required to collect and remit the sales tax to qualified states.

[In January 2001] the participating states in the Streamlined Sales Tax Project (SSTP) voted unanimously to adopt the multistate streamlined sales and use tax agreement that set the parameters for states to participate in a joint effort to simplify and modernize sales and use tax administration to substantially reduce the burden of tax compliance. Governors are now working with state legislators to set a meeting for the participating states to reach consensus on the requirements for states to join, or be ejected, from a multistate system, a system that provides for uniformity in state and local tax bases, a central electronic registration system, simplification of state and local sales tax rates, and terms for certified service providers. The new system will include a number of uniform definitions, including for food and clothing, and set forth states' policy for the protection of privacy. Since January 2001, 16 Governors have signed streamlined enabling legislation into law. . . .

Governors recognize that the transformation of the patchwork state and local sales tax system to streamline it for the new economy cannot be accomplished by states alone. The federal government must be a partner in encouraging and providing incentives for this unprecedented undertaking—one that will be far easier to block than enable. . . . The Governors believe that the 32 participating states in the Streamlined Sales Tax Project have a unique opportunity to work together with Congress to enact a twenty-first century sales tax that will ensure states are prepared to support the global electronic marketplace. With estimates that one-third of the $8 trillion national economy could be conducted electronically over the course of the decade, we believe that all parties should compete—as they do under the federal Internet tax system—on a level playing field. [Editor's note: As of March 2002, streamlined sales tax legislation has been passed in fifteen states but has not been taken up at the federal level.]

Government Regulation of the Internet Harms Society

by Jamie Dettmer

About the author: *Jamie Dettmer is senior editor of* Insight on the News *magazine.*

Maybe writing a lament for the freewheeling ways of the Internet would be premature. After all, the battle to protect the freedom of cyberspace from regulatory interference hardly has commenced, and taxes have not yet been imposed on e-sales in either the United States or Europe. But already there are those lusting to tame the wild of cyberspace with the lassos and hobbles of government control and taxes.

Here in the United States most of the nation's governors are intensifying their campaigns to get Congress to approve a sales tax on Internet commerce. [In fall 2001] all House and Senate members received a letter from 40 governors urging that there be no extension of a 1998 moratorium on Internet taxes.

The governors argue that it isn't fair to tax brick-and-mortar stores while allowing trade to be conducted untaxed online—the e-businesses have a commercial advantage, they say. Advocates of a tax-free Internet maintain that imposing taxes now could snuff out the e-commerce sector and that with more than 7,000 tax jurisdictions around, it will become burdensome for online traders to identify who should pay what and when. Others are demanding a streamlined national online-sales tax.

Chances are that this time a failure to come up with a workable compromise will result in Congress extending the moratorium when it returns from the summer recess. [In November 2001, President Bush signed a law extending the Internet sales tax moratorium through 2003.] But few on Capitol Hill believe the Internet will remain a tax-free zone for long, especially as development continues apace of new technologies that enable the location of users to be identified.

In some ways the Internet has been too successful for its own good. The development of technologies to speed content delivery, protect networks from hackers and intruders, or target advertising based on a user's location slowly but surely are being exploited by authorities worldwide to housebreak the Internet. The great libertarian hopes that cyberspace would be beyond the reach of interfering regulators or authoritarian regimes are increasingly in danger of being dashed.

Those who worry that the Internet is being exploited by pornographers and organized-crime networks tend to welcome increasing regulation to snoop and detect. But the other side warns that the full liberating power of the Internet already is at risk of being blunted by such activity.

Putting Chains on Cyberspace

Once it was argued that the free flow of information on the Internet would hasten the demise of dictators and closed regimes in much the same way that Radio Liberty, the Voice of America and the BBC World Service helped undermine communism in Russia and Eastern Europe. Now the same geo-location technologies developed to further the efficiency of the Internet and exploit its commercial potential are being used by the Chinese government, for example, to filter out information it doesn't like and doesn't want its people to see.

> *"The great libertarian hopes that cyberspace would be beyond the reach of interfering regulators or authoritarian regimes are increasingly in danger of being dashed."*

According to the Washington-based Carnegie Endowment for International Peace (CEIP), Beijing has limited online political discourse by firewalling the country and filtering the flow of Internet traffic in and out, preventing the Chinese people from accessing particular Websites. Filtering likewise is taking place in Singapore, Saudi Arabia and Iran. As the CEIP concluded in a recent report: "The diffusion of the Internet does not necessarily spell the demise of authoritarian rule."

The free-floating Internet has lost its wings—gravity has brought it down to earth, enabling the geography of politics to reassert itself and to dictate what people can view or even buy. The effect is chilling.

[The November 2000] court decision in France ordering Yahoo! to prevent French users from purchasing Nazi memorabilia—banned in France—on the face of it was a cheering ruling and a reassertion of national sovereignty and the right of states to enforce local laws. But the result has been to force a cautious Yahoo! to pull worldwide all such items from sale on its auction Website, meaning French law is being allowed to dictate to others.

Even more disturbing, authorities in the United States and Europe appear eager to snoop on Internet users, arguing that criminals and terrorists abound and can advance their evil designs on the Internet.

Britain has followed the example of Vladimir Putin's Russia. It now requires that Internet-access providers hot-wire to the intelligence services, allowing them to read any e-mail or peer at any e-commerce that goes through providers based in Britain. As in Russia, a warrant, or government permission, will be required before the snoops are allowed to snoop, but the history of abused warrants for phone-tapping in the United Kingdom hardly inspires confidence.

The claim leveled to justify the hot-wiring—namely that it allows security forces to spy on the bad guys and gain information about what they are up to—is suspect. It is the bad guys who can afford to purchase and develop encryption technology. The Mexican drug kingpins, for example, employ computer scientists recently graduated from North American universities to help them secure their e-mails from prying eyes. Drug Enforcement Administration sources tell political notebook that the drug barons' use of the Internet is highly sophisticated.

Cyberlibertarians fear that this sudden reassertion of regulators and the cloak-and-dagger brigade likely will have two long-term effects on the Internet—to Balkanize [divide] it and to make it far more timid.

Stronger Internet Privacy Laws Are Unnecessary

by Maureen Sirhal

About the author: *Maureen Sirhal is a reporter for the* National Journal.

By now, it's a cliché to say that the Internet raises privacy concerns. The instantaneous nature and global reach of the Web, and the ease with which consumers can be tracked, classified, and marketed to, have raised worries about privacy to new heights.

On one level, this is understandable. Thanks to advances in information gathering, law enforcement groups and government agencies can now pilfer through millions of bits of data in seconds without anyone knowing what's happening. Technical tools like Web bugs and cookies leave behind electronic footprints that retailers and marketers use to compile consumer profiles, often without the knowledge or consent of the shopper. The seemingly endless barrage of news stories about the unsavory Web surfing habits of celebrities, businessmen, or politicians further drives the point home.

Yet in the 20-plus years since Congress made its first foray into the politics of privacy, not much has changed. While the Internet speeds the exchange of information—information that has become more detailed with each year—the selling of consumer data has long been standard practice in retailing, back to the days when "cookies" and "spam" were still things that people ate.

In the policy debate about privacy, consumers are left with little understanding of the tradeoff between the forced cost of providing "privacy" and the very real benefits of information sharing. The debate over privacy has created a major hurdle for businesses as they move to utilize the information superhighway to create convenience for consumers, all of which adds unnecessary costs to a mechanism that has revolutionized—and extended worldwide—the free market.

Privacy vs. Convenience

Given the rise in Internet usage and its prevalence in daily culture, it's no shock that Internet-related privacy concerns are close to universal. But even in the days before widespread access to the Internet, consumers had doubts about the integration of personal privacy and technology. In 1992, a Harris-Equifax survey on technology issues found that "most Americans acknowledge that computers have brought benefits to society, yet they still consider some uses of computers threats to personal privacy." Eighty-nine percent of respondents agreed that "computers give people more convenient access to useful information and services." But 68 percent agreed that "the present uses of computers represent a threat to personal privacy." Nearly ten years later, the numbers haven't changed much.

That's because the same type of consumer data have been compiled for years by companies like American Express, which then sells the information to marketers. Indeed, magazine lists are great sources for consumer data for many of the same reasons. More than any other medium, a consumer's choice of magazines can tell a lot about "what a person likes, his or her interests, etc.," wrote Michael Pashby, executive vice president of the Magazine Publishers of America, in public comments to the Federal Trade Commission.

The fact is, people demonstrate mixed behavior when it comes to privacy. When asked, "Is privacy important to you?" the vast majority of Americans answer yes. Yet they do little to maintain their privacy in the face of marketers who seek to know everything about them. They fear identity theft but are often willing to give away vital information—including name, address, date of birth, and Social Security number—in exchange for deep discounts on the Web. They express disdain for marketers yet will gladly apply for a "savings card" at the local grocery store, knowing how important that information will be to retailers.

Consider some preliminary statistics offered by Don Ogilvie, executive vice president of the American Bankers Association. Speaking before a privacy conference organized by the National Center for Policy Analysis, Ogilvie confirmed that few consumers responded to mandatory notices that all financial service institutions were required to send to customers disclosing their information-gathering practices. Under the recently-passed Graham-Leach-Bliley financial deregulation legislation, financial services companies must inform consumers how their personal information will be used once a company collects it. The notice provides a mechanism for consumers to opt out of any information-sharing.

> *"Once you get beyond simple questions about 'concern' over privacy, most consumers are really concerned about convenience."*

According to Ogilvie, "The little sketchy information that we've gotten from some of the banks . . . is that . . . 1 to 2 percent [of consumers] are opting out." That's less than even the predicted rate of 5 percent.

It turns out, once you get beyond simple questions about "concern" over privacy, most consumers are really concerned about convenience. Recently, Earth-Link Internet Services kicked off an advertising campaign touting its commitment to consumer privacy that resulted in major attention for the company. And what was the number one "privacy concern" consumers reported, according to EarthLink executive Les Seagraves? Spam email.

The Costs of Privacy

So the hue and cry over Internet privacy may seem a bit overblown when you consider what people actually do. Not that we should entirely discount the dangers of the Internet when it comes to privacy. Identity theft, for example, is on a rapid increase, according to the Treasury Department's Financial Crimes Enforcement Network (FinCen), in large part because of the proliferation of information on the Web and potential for bad actors to use Web sites to trade information. But even FinCen noted in its report that the most common cause of identity theft remains "loss or theft of a purse or wallet, mail theft, and fraudulent address changes."

But is this good enough reason for Uncle Sam to construct a new system of laws and regulations to protect online privacy? Consider this: despite the ramblings from Capitol Hill about the need to regulate e-commerce, the U.S. government ranks as one of the biggest privacy violators. A recent GAO report revealed that barely half of all federal agencies have complied

> *"The average person has far more privacy today than a century ago."*

with a mandatory rule to remove from their Web sites electronic cookies that were used to track user information. Indeed, the Office of National Drug Control Policy continues to use information harvested by its Web site cookies to tailor anti-drug marketing campaigns.

There will be one clear outcome if extensive new privacy protections are enacted: prices will rise, for purchases both on- and offline. The selling of consumer information has been going on for years and has helped to offset product prices and modernize the country's consumer-related retailers and industries. Consumer information allows retailers to target advertising campaigns—studies have shown that it can increase marketing effectiveness tenfold and more—with those savings passed on to consumers. And new regulations will only increase the cost of compliance and ultimately the cost of goods.

Privacy rules will do more than raise the price of a book at Amazon.com. Consider how costs in areas like health care will be affected. Already, doctors and medical experts have noted that the costs of upgrading health care systems to implement new privacy rules will run into the billions of dollars.

The rules, if unchanged, would require an annoying scheme of duplicative consent forms for the transferring for medical information. Consumers can forget about having the drugstore deliver their weekly medication if they have not first supplied written consent to the pharmacy to allow their doctor to phone in a prescription.

And of course, new regulations will only increase opportunities for the class-action lawsuits that have become a major factor in rising costs across all industries. Already, several advocacy groups have emerged to act as public guardians for privacy concerns. Twice, the Electronic Privacy and Information Center has filed complaints with the Federal Trade Commission over Amazon.com's vacillating privacy policy (the company reneged on an earlier pledge that it would not sell customer information). In both cases, the FTC found no wrongdoing on the company's part, but Amazon was forced to bear the costs of defending itself.

> *"Privacy regulations are a way for people to avoid accountability for their actions."*

Unwarranted Hysteria

Speaking at a recent conference, Federal Trade Commissioner Thomas Leary said, "In my view, there's a new hysteria on this question of privacy. People are beating the drum, and my sense is that the average person has far more privacy today than a century ago."

This is undeniably true, yet big business and the Internet have been morphed into the anonymous Big Brothers that are required in the cheap dramas that politicians love. It's a story that pulls some very deep heartstrings in the American psyche, with its devotion to liberty and freedom. The very idea that a fraudulent person, a faceless corporation, or a government agent is snooping tends to enrage Americans.

The fact is, though, that privacy regulations are a way for people to avoid accountability for their actions. If consumers are truly worried about a 24/7 marketing model, they have the power to stop doing business with whomever they choose. If they don't like banks sharing information about them with marketers, they can opt out. If they don't like companies snooping through their email or investigating their hard drives for pornography, they can send personal email at home or get their porn elsewhere. If they don't take advantage of the privacy protections that are already available to them, well, let the consumer beware.

In a culture where convenience has become the new American religion, few consumers are likely to demand stricter privacy protections if it means paying a higher price for merchandise.

Consumers ought to be wary of bad actors over the Internet, but fraud is still fraud. In cases where consumer information is abused, individuals can seek recourse through fraud statutes—and some of those may require tweaking. But the onerous scheme of required consents and regulations envisioned by many privacy advocates will lead to increased prices for all goods, decrease access to the information contained on the Web, and stifle the innovative freedom of the Internet.

In the United States, the key to prosperity has been the recognition that economic freedom promotes growth—including freedom from onerous regulatory schemes whose benefits could be fleeting. Added regulation and consumer protection on the Internet can only be increased at the expense of many of the free-wheeling qualities of the Internet, qualities that made it as integral to modern life as it is. It may not be a trade most people are willing to make.

Government Efforts to Protect Children from Online Pornography Are Ineffective

by Rob Reilly

About the author: *Rob Reilly is a computer education teacher at the Lanesborough School in Lanesborough, Massachusetts.*

As I sit here working on this article I have the television on to keep me company. I'm watching a History Channel program about the Battle of Midway. It reminds me of all those military fliers who were shot down and looked to their "shark repellent" packets to keep them safe. As my mind wanders further away from this article, I recall a college biology class where the professor went on and on about how "shark repellent" did not actually work. He talked about how so many people came to believe that it actually did work—after all, there were lots of aircrew members who were shot down into the sea, used their "shark repellent," and could testify to the fact that it worked. But the one glaring problem here is that no one was alive who could dispute the fact that it was effective.

However I must admit that "shark repellent" was a great concept. Everyone accepted it as an article of faith . . . but its actual effectiveness is in doubt. I mention this here as we seem to be facing another "shark repellent" issue—that being congressional attempts to mandate that filters be put in place to protect children from inappropriate Internet material. It seems to me that blocking software (filtering software) may be the "shark repellent" of today. . . .

The most recent congressional attempt to regulate the Web is the "Children's Internet Protection Act" (CIPA also referred to as CHIPA). This Act took effect [in April 2001]. Its purpose is to protect children from inappropriate material that exists on the Web. This legislation mandates that public libraries receiving E-Rate or Library Services Technology Act (LSTA) funds certify that "technology protection measures" are in place on "any of its computers with Internet access" and "during any use of such computers." This is certainly a noble cause. After all who could be against protecting children from bad things?

But there is opposition to this legislation. Hmmm . . . what could be wrong here? After all, we are protecting children, aren't we? Why would anyone hesitate to support protecting children from bad things?

Well . . . protecting the children is not the issue!

Congress's Third Attempt to Censor the Internet

CIPA is actually the third time around for Congress in its attempt to "protect children from inappropriate things on the Web." In recent years Congress has created the Communications Decency Act (CDA), and that was followed by the Children's Online Protection Act (COPA). Both Acts were aimed at protecting children from the evils that can be found on the Web. There are evil things on the Web and the children need to be protected—this is not in dispute. But Congress seems particularly lacking in its ability to craft a law that will perform as advertised.

"Filters just do not work properly."

The Communications Decency Act (CDA), which is suspiciously similar to CIPA and to COPA, was ruled to be unconstitutional by the Supreme Court in a 9 to 0 vote. The CDA was vague and overly broad, it violated the constitutional rights of adults, it unconstitutionally restricted protected speech, etc. etc. etc. So now we are left with COPA and CIPA or CDA II and CD III if you'd prefer.

And here we go with round two. In May 2001 the Supreme Court announced that it will hear arguments in regard to the Children's Online Protection Act (COPA). Shari Steele, the Executive Director of the Electronic Frontier Foundation (EFF), states, "COPA is just as unconstitutional now as when federal courts struck it down in 1999 and again in 2000." Steele continues, "We are pleased the United States Supreme Court has agreed to hear the case so that COPA can follow its predecessor, the Communications Decency Act, into the dustbin of history." [As of March 2002, the case is still before the Court.]

But the adventure continues. This is like watching Wiley Coyote continually try to overcome various immutable laws of physics and catch the Road Runner.

Like its predecessor the CDA, both COPA and CIPA do the following:
• Restrict adult access to material as well as minors.
• Override local decision-making and control.
• Unconstitutionally limit free speech.
• Are unconstitutionally broad in mandate.
• Remove speech from the Internet without any judicial determination.
• Violate constitutionally protected anonymity and privacy.
• Require adults to obtain permission in order to view blocked sites.

The prospects of the COPA being struck down are high in light of Third Circuit Court of Appeals upholding an injunction against it because, as the Court said, "We are confident that the ACLU's attack on COPA's constitutionality is likely to succeed on the merits." And based upon other previous court decisions, it would seem a safe bet that COPA and then CIPA will go the way of the CDA. But strange as it may seem, this is not even the issue as I see it. It is also not even an issue, at this point, that our Congress is trying to create laws for a global medium.

Setting legal matters aside for a moment, let me hasten to point out that there is a technology issue that is more far-reaching than the inherent legal issues I have touched upon.

The Failure of Filters

This technology issue is one that is critical whether or not you believe that filtering is a form of censorship, or, whether or not you believe that filtering to protect the children is more important than the constitutional rights of adults.

Technology protection measures do not work.

Simply put, CIPA and COPA will be ineffective because there is no technology available that can implement their mandates.

Similar to CDA and COPA, CIPA defines a "technology protection measure" as a "specific technology that blocks or filters Internet access to the material covered by certification" requirement. CIPA requires blocking of material that falls into the "obscene," "child pornography," or "harmful to minors" category. The problem is that it is not possible to create a "technology protection measure" that blocks access only to material that falls into the "obscene," "child pornography," or "harmful to minors" categories. There is no reliable way to block out objectionable material, so any "technology protection measure" will be ineffective in removing objectionable material from view. CDA could not filter appropriately and was struck down. COPA and CIPA both do what CDA did and I expect that they will be struck down.

Filters just do not work properly. This was verified in the March 2001 issue of *Consumer Reports*. A report entitled "Digital Chaperones for Kids" states that most blocking/filtering software failed to block at least 20 percent of objectionable material.

"Filtering software . . . blocks many sites . . . that are . . . clearly protected under the First Amendment."

The federal government has repeatedly found flaws in filtering programs. The U.S. Attorney General has said that filtering programs inescapably fail to block objectionable speech because they are unable to screen for images (refer to the Brief for the Appellants, Reno v. ACLU, No. 96-511 (January 1997) pages 40–41). Even a congressional report has found that filtering software is "not the preferred solution" given the risk that "protected, harmless, or innocent speech would be accidentally or inappropriately blocked" (refer to H.R. Rep. No. 105-775 (1998) page 19).

In 1998, the Child Online Protection Act Commission ("COPA Commission") was created by Congress. Its mandate was to "identify technological or other methods that will help reduce access by minors to material that is harmful to minors on the Internet." In October 2000, the COPA Commission reported that filtering "technology raises First Amendment concerns because of its potential to be over-inclusive in blocking content. Concerns are increased because the extent of blocking is often unclear and not disclosed and may not be based on parental choices." Also noteworthy was the fact that the Commission did not recommend any mandatory use of filtering technologies.

> *"Congress fails to protect children by failing to realize that no filtering software or blocking mechanism is completely effective."*

In October 2000, Peacefire, an organization created to represent the interests of people under 18 in the debate regarding speech on the Internet, issued a report on blocking technology. This report found error rates that ranged from 20 to 80 percent. These error rates were based on blocking software that identified non-pornographic sites as being pornographic.

Another interesting report came from The Internet Filter Assessment Project (TIFAP). This group is composed of concerned librarians who were interested in the use of filters in libraries. The TIFAP director, Karen G. Schneider notes, "Some of the volunteers were 'pro' some were 'anti,' some were uncertain, but all were of the mindset that you don't know a tool until you use it.". . .

The Other Side of the Coin

Filtering software not only fails to effectively block "harmful" material, but it blocks many sites and material that are not objectionable (and clearly protected under the First Amendment).

This over-blocking of material causes difficulty in retrieving acceptable material. For example, searching for material on "Mars exploration" would be blocked as the last letter of the word "Mars" and the first two letters of "exploration" create a blocked word. Also searches for recent information about the NFL Super Bowls would be blocked (hint: Super Bowl XXX contains a blocked term). Searches for information on "breast cancer" have a good possibility of being blocked, as part of the phrase contains a blocked word. Then there is Jamie McKenzie's online magazine, *From Now On,* which was blocked by several vendors because Jamie wrote an article about the dangers of the Web. His article contained certain terms that were on vendors' block lists. Well, I certainly hope that this magazine is not blocked due to this article containing several blocked terms. But you may ask, "How can this happen?" Good question!

When conducting a routine search, Yahoo!, AltaVista, Snap, and other search engines search the Web by scanning the Web pages for various words, terms, phrases, etc. Search engines then catalog this information so that a user may search for a given term or phrase. When the search engine finds the phrase or term, it points the user to that Web address. Filtering software does much the same thing, except filtering software creates a list of blocked sites and when it comes across words, phrases, and terms that are considered by the vendor as inappropriate, it blocks the user from accessing that site or Web page.

After using this technology to identify Web sites to block, the blocking program vendors add these pages to a master list of Web pages to block ("blocked sites list"). Some vendors claim to have employees review individual Web sites before adding them to the blocked site list. Even if we believe that there are employees screening Web sites, these employees are not lawyers or judges, and receive no legal training. As a result, untrained employees are making legal decisions and excluding constitutionally protected material.

As American Civil Liberties Union (ACLU) Legislative Counsel Marvin Johnson states: "Because of the way these blocking programs work, they inherently rely upon the exercise of subjective human judgment by the vendor to decide what is objectionable and what is not. The vendor, rather than librarians, other government officials, adult patrons, or parents, decide what gets placed on the 'blocked sites' list."

Johnson continues, "Furthermore, because of the massive amounts of information available on the Web, and its constantly changing content, no company can keep up with all the information or changes. It is estimated that even the most sophisticated search techniques find less than 20 percent [of material that exists] on the Web. Therefore, the idea that blocking technology will block out all of the objectionable information on the Web is an impossibility. Although blocking program vendors provide updates to their blocked sites list, it is impossible for them to find all of the content on the Internet that meets their criteria, or to keep up with the rapidly increasing and changing content available."

No Quick Fix for a Complex Problem

Protecting children is a very laudable goal. However, Congress fails to protect children by failing to realize that no filtering software or blocking mechanism is completely effective. But it would seem that even if COPA and CIPA are ruled unconstitutional, Congress will act again.

Congress fails to realize, or just plainly ignores, the fact that it's a technology problem at this moment. Congress also fails to understand that it is trying to create laws for a global medium. But even if the technology were available to block/filter in accordance with COPA and CIPA, the issue would next become one of identifying the context in which the word or phrase is used. And that issue is not a technology issue, it is, and always will be, a legal issue . . . technology will not solve this context issue, which is at the crux of this situation.

State Governments Should Not Be Able to Tax E-Commerce

by Edwin Feulner

About the author: *Edwin Feulner is president of the Heritage Foundation, a conservative public policy think tank in Washington, D.C.*

I've studied government policy for more than 30 years, and if I know one thing, it's this: Lawmakers will tax just about anything.

From pets to pornography, examples run the gamut. The federal government taxes unemployment benefits. The burial fees in many local jurisdictions include a "cadaver fee." In Los Angeles County, politicians want a local electronics company to pay a property tax on the satellites they've launched—ones now floating some 22,000 miles above the Earth.

So I'm not surprised to learn that 40 of the nation's governors are urging Congress to allow them to tax Internet purchases. With the federal moratorium on Internet taxes slated to end October 21, 2001, states facing tighter budgets are looking at Internet taxes the way a fat man on a diet looks at an ice-cream sundae.

And if they can pull it off, the states could net an extra $30 billion by 2003, Governor Jim Geringer, R-Wyoming, recently told the National Governors Association.

Of course, they're all eyeing the same sundae—and they all want it made differently. There are about 30,000 tax jurisdictions in the United States, and 7,500 of them levy sales taxes. Few, if any, impose those taxes the same way on the same things.

The Practical Problems of an E-Tax

Washington, D.C. once had a popcorn tax that applied to popped popcorn but not to unpopped kernels. Florida taxes charcoal if it's used for cookouts, but not if it's used for gardening. You can imagine how the hair-splitting nuances of tax policy could create a mess for Internet businesses, which offer everything from pants to peacocks to Porsches.

Another problem with an Internet tax is the question of who can be taxed in the first place. Both the Supreme Court and the Constitution say that states can impose sales taxes on companies and people in their borders. But with the Internet, it's possible to buy something from a business in Hawaii without leaving your home in Maine. So who pays the sales tax? The company in Hawaii? The buyer in Maine? Neither?

Unfortunately, many governors think the answer should be "both." They've already proposed something called the Streamlined Sales Tax Project, which they say would "simplify" state and local tax definitions, exemptions and rates. But it's really a step toward a national sales tax, which is hardly something Americans need, considering the number of taxes they already pay, from sales taxes, income taxes and property taxes to death taxes, payroll taxes and so-called "sin" taxes.

> *"E-taxes would spoil perhaps the greatest business development since the creation of money."*

If states *must* impose Internet sales tax, they should follow the examples of catalog companies, which tax only people who live in the same state as the businesses they're buying from. After all, the Internet is essentially a catalog that moves at the speed of a mouse click.

But the best solution would be to make the moratorium permanent. E-taxes would spoil perhaps the greatest business development since the creation of money. Thanks to the Internet, you can buy anything, anytime, anywhere in a marketplace bigger than anything even the great economist Adam Smith could have dreamed of.

Now 40 governors want to spoil this great multibillion-dollar economic marketplace. They may call it a matter of fairness, but it sounds more like an old-fashioned money grab.

Chapter 4

What Is the Future of the Information Age?

Chapter Preface

In her 2001 book *The Death of Distance: How the Communications Revolution Is Changing Our Lives*, Frances Cairncross makes a number of predictions about the future of the Information Age. "The death of distance and the communications revolution will be among the most important forces shaping economies and societies in the next fifty years," she writes. More specifically, she predicts that "the Internet will change electronic products of all kinds, from television and the telephone to games and cameras"; that "for consumers everywhere, electronic commerce will eventually bring empowerment: to search, to bargain, to specify"; and that the Information Revolution "will, on balance, be a force for peace. . . . The best way to discourage countries from fighting one another is surely through better communication."

Cairncross's forecasts are modest compared with some of the claims that have been made about the Information Age. Particularly in the early 1990s, when Americans were being introduced to e-mail and the World Wide Web, some technology gurus predicted that the Internet would unite the world into one shared culture and render national borders meaningless. The temptation to make bold predictions about the Information Age is still strong: In 1999, there was a flurry of news stories reporting that Napster, a software program that lets people share music files over the Internet, would lead to the death of the major recording studios and copyright law in general.

In response to such predictions, a plethora of critics have emerged to debunk the wilder claims about the Internet. A 2000 editorial in the *Economist* is typical:

> Even when everyone on the planet has been connected to the Internet, there will still be wars, and pollution, and inequality. As new gizmos come and go, human nature seems to remain stubbornly unchanged; despite the claims of the techno-prophets, humanity cannot simply invent away its failings. The Internet is not the first technology to have been hailed as a panacea—and it will certainly not be the last.

While it is important to be wary of wild or unfounded predictions about information technology, one should also keep an open mind about where the Information Age is headed. The old adage that change is inevitable pertains to both technology and modern society. The viewpoints in the following chapter offer a variety of perspectives on the future of the Information Age.

The Information Age May Make Traditional Universities Obsolete

by Samuel L. Dunn

About the author: *Samuel L. Dunn is vice president for academic affairs and a professor of business and mathematics at Northwest Nazarene University.*

By 2025, traditional universities may be a thing of the past, replaced by consortia of course providers with delivery systems that simply bypass the classroom.

Education is an absolute imperative in the emerging global knowledge society, so new ways of providing access to education for a much higher percentage of the population are now being devised.

The most dramatic examples of access to education are found in the 11 distance-education mega-universities found around the world. In "distance education," the student is separated in time or space from the teacher or professor. The largest of these high enrollment universities is in China, the China Central Radio and Television University, with more than 3 million students. The English-speaking world has the British Open University, with 215,000 students, and the University of South Africa, with 120,000 students. In addition to the mega-universities, dozens of other national and regional systems are providing education at all levels to students. The Open University of Hong Kong, Universidade Aberta (Portugal), the Universidad Nacional de Education a Distancia (Spain), and the recently formed Western Governors University (United States) are just a few of those providing lower and/or higher education to needy citizenry.

Learning from Afar

The base delivery system for the distance-education mega-universities is television, supplemented by other technologies or even some onsite instruction in more-developed countries. Some distance-education systems use two-way interactive video connections to particular locations where students gather; others

Excerpted from "The Virtualizing of Education," by Samuel L. Dunn, *Futurist*, March 2000. Copyright © 2000 by World Future Society. Reprinted with permission.

supplement with the Internet, and still others deliver only by Internet. With video- and audio-streaming now available, the Internet appears to be the technology of choice for systems where students have access to computers. Of course, these technologies merely add to the radio-delivered courses that have been offered for years in many countries around the world.

The programs and courses offered vary from basic literacy courses to the highest graduate-level programming. Hundreds of university degrees are now available through distance education, where 90% or more of the required credits are given at a distance, as are dozens of master's degrees and a small number of accredited doctoral degrees. One estimate suggests that 50,000 university-level courses are now available through distance-education delivery systems.

How will distance education affect traditional schools and universities? Primary and secondary schools have been a standard in most of the English-speaking world for at least a century. A large installed base of higher-education institutions provides adult and postsecondary educational services to students. In the United States, there are more than 3,600 accredited institutions of higher education, about half public and half independent. In addition, there are about the same number of other kinds of schools, colleges, and institutes that have access to federal funding for their students. The United Kingdom has approximately 120 recognized universities and hundreds of other educational institutions. It would seem that such a large installed base of traditional universities and schools would not be threatened by the new distribution channels of the knowledge society, but threatened they are.

> *"I predict that 10% of existing public colleges and 50% of independent colleges will close in the next 25 years."*

Management theorist Peter Drucker has predicted that traditional universities as we know them will become a big wasteland in the next 25 years. The Association of Governing Boards predicts that one-third of the existing independent colleges and universities in the United States will close in the next 10 years.

I predict that 10% of existing public colleges and 50% of independent colleges will close in the next 25 years. Almost all colleges will be radically reshaped by the digital revolution.

The Virtual Student Body

The shape of the future of higher education in North America and Europe is starting to be visible. One of the most important features is that boundaries of time and space are being eliminated. When students had to go to a particular location to access their educational programs, it made sense to talk about regional accreditation, tuition areas, service regions, and semesters. The new delivery systems antiquate these notions. With asynchronous delivery on the Internet, for example, the same course can be taken by a student in Hong Kong or Helsinki,

Pretoria or Peoria. These changes in delivery will make it necessary to develop new ways of accrediting or approving courses and programs that students may receive from many parts of the world.

There will be two main types of educational institutions: those that add value in coursework and those that are certifying agencies. The certifying colleges and universities are those that act as educational bankers for students. Students will earn credits from many places and have the credits or certifications of completion sent to

> *"Almost all courses in the residential college of the future will be digitally enhanced."*

the certifying university, then that certifying university will award the degree when enough credits of the right type have been accumulated. Regent's College of the University of the State of New York and Thomas Edison College of New Jersey are public certifying institutions that give accredited degrees.

One vision for some of the remaining residential colleges in the United States, now serving mainly the 18- to 23-year-old population, is that many will become certifying colleges. Students will come to the colleges for their social, artistic, athletic, and spiritual programs. The basic commodity these colleges will sell is membership in the college community. Students will access their courses from colleges and universities around the world, transfer the credits to the college, then gain a degree. Faculty members will serve as tutors and advisers and may provide some courses live.

Most traditional colleges and universities already could be classified as certifying institutions. With more than 50% of all college graduates studying in more than one institution before graduating, most colleges readily accept the courses that are transferred in from other accredited institutions. In a majority of institutions, even now, a student has to take only one year of credits from that institution to get a degree.

The distinction between distance education and local education will become blurred. Almost all courses in the residential college of the future will be digitally enhanced. Because distance-education methodologies provide some advantages to student learning, those techniques will be incorporated into local teaching. By the year 2025, at least 95% of instruction in the United States will be digitally enhanced.

Digital courseware for most college-level courses will be available much sooner than 2025. Studies have shown that there are 25 college-level courses that get about 50% of the total credit enrollment across U.S. higher education. Among these are Introduction to Psychology, U.S. History, Introduction to English Composition, Statistics, Introductory Spanish, and Calculus. There will be "killer applications" for these 25 courses available by 2010. These killer apps—so-called because of their quality, their comprehensive character, and their widespread usage—will be available for both distance and local usage. Courseware publishers will realize huge profits from these applications.

As we make the transition to the new world of education, thousands of organizations will develop their own digitized courseware, thus reinventing the wheel over and over again. However, a general shakeout of courseware developers will leave a small number of courseware consortia and companies that will provide the bulk of courseware. These groups will sell courses directly to students and license courseware to colleges and universities.

While the number of traditional educational institutions will go down, the number of providers of higher education will increase. The 7,000 current providers recognized by the U.S. Department of Education will grow to 10,000 by the year 2025. Publishers, corporations, for-profit and nonprofit entities will get into the education business, because there is big money to be made. Publishers will sell courses directly to students and thus eliminate the university middleman. The present 1,000 corporate universities will double by 2025.

Money is big in education. The United States alone spends $600 billion on education of all types each year, making it the second largest industry after health care. With estimates that the typical citizen will need the equivalent of 30 semester credits of coursework each 10 years to keep up with the changes that are coming, entrepreneurs see opportunities for large profits.

The need for continuing education is growing—a trend that will be compounded as the population base increases. The number of students needing traditional higher education in the United States is predicted to climb from the present 15 million to an estimated 20 million by the year 2010. Of the 6 billion people now on the globe, more than 1 billion are teenagers. It will be a gargantuan task to provide the education these people need to reap the benefits of the new world economy.

While entrepreneurs and for-profit organizations go after the profits available, governments will try to make education more efficient and save taxpayer dollars. Seamless education policies will make the transition from primary to secondary to higher education easier. Students will be encouraged to finish high school and college in six or seven years. States and provinces will provide financial incentives to institutions and directly to students to move through the system faster than normal.

> *"The virtual university has been born and is growing rapidly; it will be the predominant mode of higher education by the year 2025."*

The home-school movement will lead to the home-college movement. With the increased emphasis on educational outcomes, new systems of examinations and other assessment techniques will be made available to students who wish to study on their own. Certifying universities will provide the needed degrees and credentials.

Many independent colleges and universities will close, but there will still be a niche market for residential universities. Universities that provide a religious community or other special programming for older adolescents will still be viable and desirable. To survive, and to attract students who are willing to pay the differential price, these institutions must provide high-quality special-interest programming for the niche. Much more than coursework must be available and delivered.

Networked Education

We are moving away from the factory university, a place-bound, product-oriented institution that provides educational services—teaching, research, and service—to its clients at the time, place, and pace desired by the institution.

The virtual university is next—not a single institution, but a web of educational providers that collectively distribute services to the client at the time, place, pace, and style desired by the client, with quality determined by the client and a variety of approving and accrediting bodies. The virtual university has been born and is growing rapidly; it will be the predominant mode of higher education by the year 2025.

While higher education will enjoy the most dramatic changes, primary and secondary education will change as well. These levels of instruction will be heavily digitized in the years ahead, although more emphasis will be given to moving students out of the home in order to benefit from socialization and enculturation with live teachers and classmates.

Alternatives to the public schools will continue to grow and be more popular. Television- and Internet-delivered courseware to support home schoolers is already being written and disseminated. Increasing demands for quality will be heard and responded to by public schools, church schools, and both nonprofit and for-profit entrepreneurs.

These are exciting days in education. Education is an absolute necessity for the knowledge society. Change is rapidly altering the face of educational delivery, but one thing is sure: The English-speaking world will continue to invest large portions of its resources to assuring an educated citizenry for the future.

The Information Age Will Not Make Traditional Universities Obsolete

by A. Michael Noll

About the author: *A. Michael Noll is a professor at the Annenberg School for Communication at the University of Southern California and a senior affiliated research fellow at the Columbia Institute for Tele-Information.*

Some experts are predicting the death of the university. They claim that the Internet will make universities obsolete as students around the globe study and take courses, all on the Internet. The 'webtization' of university education will mean the end of physical universities. All education will be virtual, they say. Still other experts predict that corporations will prepare, package and sell education on such a wide scale over the Internet that conventional universities will no longer be able to compete or survive. The corporatization of education will occur on such a wide scale that it will lead to the death of conventional educational institutions. Are such dire predictions for the future of the university sensible? What will the university of the future look like?

Dire Predictions

Dire predictions have been made before. I am old enough to remember the prediction that computers would lead to a paperless office. Instead, computers made it far too easy to create many drafts, all usually printed on paper by the high-speed laser printer. I can recall predictions of the electronic library in which all information would be stored in digital form without the need for any paper books. This prediction has been extended to include the impending death of books in general. Yet book sales increase each year and hardly anyone would prefer to read a book on a computer screen. The electronic newspaper was predicted to herald the demise of conventional newspapers. Here too, the prediction was far too dire.

Excerpted from "Technology and the Future of the University," by A. Michael Noll, *Information, Communication & Society,* www.infosoc.co.uk, December 2000. Copyright © 2000 by Taylor and Francis Books. Reprinted with permission.

These kinds of dire predictions seem to be publicity stunts, designed to attract the attention of the media. Outlandish predictions of the impending death of established institutions are usually successful at receiving far more attention than they deserve. Rarely does the media remember what was predicted last year and, thus, no negative publicity returns to tarnish the image of the wild predictor when the predictions turn to rubbish.

> *"Outlandish predictions of the impending death of established institutions are usually successful at receiving far more attention than they deserve."*

How then can we understand the future better? At the end of the last century, predictions abounded as experts looked forward to the coming next century. How can we know what predictions make sense and which are nonsense?

We all know the tremendous pace of computer technology over the past 40 years and, thus, we are tempted to believe the claims that similar revolutionary change will occur to educational institutions. But a saner approach to making predictions of the future is to look back 40 years to see what has happened in the intervening years to today. This historical perspective can then be used to make more realistic extrapolations to the future. When this is done for universities, we see that very little has changed. The classroom is still the dominant technique for teaching, although computers and the Internet are much used by students for research and to register for courses.

An Old Idea

What then of distance education and the predictions that the conventional classroom will soon disappear? In fact, distance education is a very old idea. Correspondence schools have existed throughout the twentieth century. Tele-education through two-way video and one-way video, with an interactive audio return, has been available for decades and is still used by many engineering schools.

Students have studied with each other over the telephone for decades, and today use e-mail for similar purposes. The Internet is a great supplement to the library, but its use for research makes students lazy and much material is missed because it is not available over the Internet, perhaps because it is too old or simply has not been entered. Students routinely complain to me about too much emphasis on the Internet and state their desire to have access to physical books and reference materials.

Whenever I ask my students whether they want to take courses over the Internet they respond very negatively. Students do not seem to want web based courses! Students prefer the classroom and the personal interactions with other students. This is not to say that there are special circumstances for distance education over the Internet, for example, for students who are far too busy to attend physically. But this is a small market, already satisfied by correspondence schools and others specializing in distance education.

The university is—and always has been—a physical place where students, scholars and teachers come together. The university that creates a rich environment to facilitate interactions, both in and outside the formal classroom, will indeed flourish in the future. The university that emphasizes distance education and the Internet will die, because of the cold, impersonal nature of such education.

The Internet's Impact

There have been some changes, though, because of the Internet. A few years ago nearly all of our graduate students found out about our school through the use of college guides. Today, nearly all have instead used the Internet to find out about the school and its academic programmes. The Internet is a tremendous marketing tool. Faculty biographies, programme descriptions, information about graduates, course syllabi, faculty publications and even web-cams of the campus create a package of instantly-available material to help a prospective student decide where to apply. Even the application material is available over the Internet.

In the future, the Internet could have a negative impact on the university bookstore. Each term, the university's bookstore asks me to give it a list of the books required for my courses. Filling out this form takes time with no rewards to me. All too often, the bookstore forgets to order the books. Students are discovering the use of the Internet to search for a cheap price and then have the books shipped directly to them, thereby avoiding the bookstore. I too have joined this new approach and am no longer filling out the bookstore's form. Instead, I give the students a list of the books along with the suggestion that they search the Internet for the best price and delivery schedule to meet their needs, in addition to checking the university's bookstore.

> *"The university that emphasizes distance education and the Internet will die, because of the cold, impersonal nature of such education."*

The university's bookstore prepares course readers, consisting of copies of all the required readings for the course. The bookstore is making a business in obtaining permissions from the copyright owners, paying royalties and then printing the readers. Here too the Internet could facilitate much change. Many publications are available over the Internet, either for free or for a nominal charge. All the faculty would need to do is prepare a list of the readings along with the appropriate URLs on the Internet. Indeed, it is the university bookstore that would seem to have a dim future!

Online Voting Could Improve Elections

by Kevin Bonsor

About the author: *Kevin Bonsor is a writer for* HowStuffWorks, *an online educational magazine.*

Editor's Note: The following viewpoint was written in November 2000, just after the U.S. presidential election. The election was held on November 7, but for weeks after the initial voting the nation's attention was focused on a recount of Florida's ballots, the results of which would ultimately decide the election. During the recount process, it became apparent that there were many problems with the punch-card ballots used in some Florida counties: Often the holes in the ballot card did not punch through completely, so many of them had to be disqualified. The Florida recount prompted many calls for nationwide election reform.

Can you believe all of the confusion and controversy surrounding [the 2000] U.S. presidential election? Few elections have ever had this many twists and turns. In most presidential elections, our next president is usually decided before we go to bed on election night. Vice President Al Gore and Governor George W. Bush must have spent many restless nights since last week's election, thinking about the few hundreds of votes that separate the two men in Florida—votes which will decide the presidency, as Florida claims 25 Electoral College votes.

The 2000 election will always be remembered for the confusion that developed on election night and the days following. Early on election night, TV networks announced that Gore had won Florida, but then retracted that announcement. Then Florida was awarded to Bush, only for it to be announced later that the state was too close to call. Thousands of ballots were tossed out in South Florida because some voters couldn't decipher the so-called "butterfly" ballot. Disputes over just a few hundred votes are keeping one of these men from claiming the White House, and legal suits and recounts are under way to decide who our next president will be. Perhaps the most amazing thing about the entire situation is that, in what is arguably the most technologically advanced country in the world, Americans are still voting with paper ballots. Little progress has been made since the American fore- fathers dropped beans in a jar to cast their votes.

We have the technology today to perform computerized elections. In fact, some companies, universities and unions already use e-voting to elect their officials. . . . The next time Americans vote for the U.S. president, it might be at the breakfast table, checking off an online ballot on a PC or per- sonal digital assistant.

> *"E-voting is the next logical step for elections."*

Point and Click Voting

Americans live in a country that is heavily dependent on millions of comput- ers. . . . Computers do more than just connect us to the World Wide Web. Al- most everyone uses an ATM for a good portion of their bank transactions. Com- puters installed on gas pumps allow us to pay at the pump. We rely on computers to help us perform many everyday tasks, but there are still things we don't trust computers to do. And one of those tasks is voting. As the 2000 elec- tion plays out, many political pundits and techies argue that electronic voting, or e-voting, will prevent a lot of the problems that have put the presidential election on hold. The advantages of e-voting include:
- Streamlining the voting process.
- Preventing ballot errors and confusion.
- Increasing national voter turnout.

Most voters already use some sort of computerized voting system. Punch cards, like the ones used in the disputed Palm Beach County, Florida, precincts, are tallied by a computerized counting machine that detects the punched holes in a ballot. This form of voting has been used since the 1960s. Optical scanners are used for those voting systems that use paper and pen, to detect pen marks made on a ballot. Optical scan vote counters are not as old as punch card tech- nology, but they seem somewhat archaic compared to other technologies that we use everyday. For many, e-voting is the next logical step for elections.

In the punch card system, if you feed the same 100 ballots through the count- ing machine seven times, you get seven different vote counts. These inaccura- cies are a problem when you are counting millions of ballots, and thousands or hundreds of votes can decide the election outcome. There are two e-voting technologies available that could streamline this process, and make counting ballots as easy as hitting a key on a computer keyboard.

In Brazil and the Netherlands, many voters already use an ATM-like machine to cast their vote. Using these machines, voters gather at their traditional voting precinct and cast their ballots in a kiosk, just like the one they have always used.

This kiosk retains the privacy that voters want. Voters carry in a cartridge and place it in the e-voting computer, which displays the candidates on a touch-screen, liquid-crystal display. Unlike paper ballots, these machines display information about each candidate aside from their party affiliation, and might even display the candidate's photo so that there is less confusion over identity. A voter makes their choice for president by touching the screen. Once the voter makes a selection, a new list of candidates, for the next office on the ballot, appears on the screen. If a voter makes a mistake, such as selecting two candidates for the same office, the computer points out this error and allows the voter to correct it. Once the voter has completed the ballot, the computer allows the voter to review his or her choices before returning the cartridge to an election official.

While it's been more than a week since polls closed on the 2000 U.S. election, and we are still awaiting the final outcomes in many states, including Florida, Oregon and New Mexico, paperless ballots can be counted instantly when polls close. There is no waiting for overseas or absentee ballots, because they can be counted along with the other e-ballots. Everything is electronic, so in addition to the benefit of timeliness, there is also less concern over human error in the counting process.

Electronic polling places are considered to be a stepping stone toward Internet voting, which would allow people to vote from their home or work computer—or any computer with Internet access. Voters could

> *"Online voting eliminates the lines at polling places, and gives us the ultimate anonymous vote."*

simply point and click on the candidate they support. This type of voting has the potential to significantly increase voter turnout. In 1998, only 44.9 percent of Americans of voting age took the time to vote. Many non-voters say that the inconvenience of registering or voting is the main reason they did not cast a ballot. With e-voting, you might eventually be able to register online. Online voting eliminates the lines at polling places, and gives us the ultimate anonymous vote. If no one actually sees you vote, there is far less chance that they can know for whom you voted.

Testing E-Voting Technology

Several states were taking a close look at e-voting even before election day 2000—but the aftermath of this year's presidential election could sway them toward implementing systems in time for the 2004 vote. You may be one of the few voters who took part in one of the various pilot e-voting programs around the country. The success or failure of these test programs will play a pivotal role in determining the future of e-voting.

Approximately 350 military personnel stationed overseas, or in states far from their home polling precincts, are the first Americans to vote via the Internet. This voting program was run by the U.S. Department of Defense's Federal

Voting Assistance Program (FVAP), and is expected to be a viable replacement for absentee or mail-in votes. These military personnel were given a certificate on a floppy disk, which was inserted in a computer. That information was paired with a similar certificate at their home county, allowing the personnel to log onto the system and vote.

This past election day, Riverside County, California, conducted the first paperless voting, and it went off with few hitches. Voters used the touch-screen, ATM-like voting machines at 715 polling locations. The e-voting machines are secure, independent computers that cost about $18,000

> *"Electronic voting is the first new election technology to be introduced in years."*

each. Voters used a cartridge to record their votes, which were then read by a computer. Proponents of electronic voting say that if the computers in Riverside had been used in Florida, a recount would have been instantaneous, if it were needed at all.

Voters in San Diego and Sacramento counties in California, and in Maricopa County in Arizona had the opportunity to cast ballots in an online voting trial on election day. In this so-called "shadow vote," voters first voted using traditional methods, and then were given the choice to vote again on a computer. The second vote was not counted toward the election, but the online votes will be studied to see if this method has potential for future elections. Tabulation of the hundreds of online shadow votes took only a few seconds, while tabulation of traditional votes takes hours or days.

With problems continuing to plague the Florida ballot count, it's likely that officials will give these pilot electronic voting programs some serious consideration. However, e-voting must overcome several obstacles before it becomes widely accepted for use in national elections. In the next section, we will look at some of the legal and technological challenges facing the implementation of e-voting.

Bridging the Digital Divide

Electronic voting is the first new election technology to be introduced in years. Of course, this change doesn't come without criticism. Traditionally, people are resistant to change, even if it offers an opportunity to simplifying their lives. And to be fair, e-voting does have its drawbacks. Here are just a few:
- Computers will disenfranchise the computer illiterate, including the elderly, the poor and minorities.
- It will be very difficult to verify voters' identities.
- Computers are susceptible to attacks by computer viruses and hackers.

The digital divide is a rather new term, referring to the gap between the technology haves and have-nots. Those with computer knowledge are typically younger and more affluent than those who lack computer skills. The electronic voting system used in Riverside County has already drawn protests from minority groups who say that this computerized system intimidates voters who have limited access to computers. Studies show that whites and Asians are more computer savvy than blacks and Latinos, that younger voters have more computer knowledge than older voters and that those with money have more access to the Internet than those without money.

The Voting Rights Act of 1965 poses the biggest legal barrier to e-voting. This act called for an end to discrimination against minorities in the election process, and prohibits some states from making changes to voting procedures without federal approval. The courts could declare computer-based or Internet voting a violation of this act.

Another potential problem facing electronic or online voting will be verifying the actual identity of the person casting the ballot. Giving a 10-digit PIN number to voters is one method of deterring voter fraud; fingerprint, iris and retinal scanners could also verify that you are who you say you are when you vote. This would be a significant improvement over the identification process used at polling places now. On election day this year, all that most of us had to do to verify our identities was recite our address. We didn't have to show any form of identification or proof of who we are.

Many people worry that voting on a computer network may make their votes vulnerable to attacks by hackers. Security measures developed to protect other areas of the Internet, including shopping, have not been able to completely lock out malicious attacks. You've probably heard of cases in which someone's credit card number was stolen online, costing the credit card holder hundreds, if not thousands, of dollars. So how can we be sure that our votes are secure? Security may be the weak link of online voting. Before e-voting becomes commonplace, developers will need to address the prospect of hackers jamming an e-voting computer system and preventing selected groups of voters from casting ballots.

E-voting has its share of flaws, but it might draw more interest following the problems that have plagued this year's election. In a country that relies so much on technology, we might finally see that technology easing the political process in the next presidential election. Who knows? In November 2004, you could wake up on election day and cast your ballot at a virtual polling booth in the privacy of your own home.

Online Voting Would Harm the Political Process

by Jonah Goldberg

About the author: *Jonah Goldberg is the editor of the* National Review Online, *the online counterpart to the* National Review, *a weekly magazine of conservative political commentary.*

In a famous episode of *The Twilight Zone,* advanced space aliens visit Planet Earth and promise a utopia for mankind. The jubilant humans are awed by the promised technological marvels—all diseases will be cured, all desires satisfied—and board spaceships in droves. A lone skeptical scientist discovers—too late—that the aliens' how-to manual, *To Serve Man,* is not actually a guide to helping humanity, but "a cookbook! It's a cookbook!"

This is not an inaccurate caricature for the occasional plight of conservatives. Every so often, a miraculous new technology comes along that requires that someone pay close attention to its downside. The Internet is just such an innovation.

The digital revolution has been wonderful for humanity. But just as the automobile unraveled many traditional communities, the World Wide Web poses a serious threat to the constitutional order—because the border-jumping nature of e-commerce is erasing our traditional conceptions of the role of government. For example, the "choice of law" movement, championed by leading Internet corporations like America Online, asserts that consumers should be allowed to decide whose laws—on tax, consumer protection, obscenity, what-have-you—should apply to their Internet transactions. If an American consumer is willing to take the risk, he should be allowed to buy Albanian medicine, Mexican food, and Dutch (ahem) "literature"—and the supplier-nation's tax and safety laws should apply. The blow to traditional sovereignties is obvious, but there are compensations: lower prices and increased choice.

More dangerous and disturbing is the push for the amorphously defined "cyber-democracy." If by cyber-democracy, one means the better and faster dissemination of political information, conservatives should applaud it. Anything that breaks the liberal media monopoly, and helps people educate themselves, is great. But if cyber-democracy means "online voting," then it would be a disaster.

Small-"d" democrats have been trying to implement cyber-democracy for several years. Last month, Iowa tested a new online voting system in polling stations. The U.S. Army is experimenting with allowing overseas servicemen to vote online. In Washington state, several local elections have been held online. California, Florida, and Minnesota are officially considering online voting on both candidates and ballot initiatives.

The Internet is taking the baton from the absentee-ballot movement. Already, twenty states have virtually no restrictions on mail-in voting. Voters can send in their ballots anytime

> *"If cyber-democracy means 'online voting,' then it would be a disaster."*

after they receive them. In Oregon, all voting is by mail—and Michigan and Ohio are considering similar systems. The logic of mail and Internet voting is simple: Voting is a good in itself, and voter turnout is disturbingly low; anything, therefore, which makes it easier for people to vote, is good—pure and simple.

"American families increasingly find it difficult to take time from their busy work schedules, child care and community activities to vote," Representative Jesse Jackson Jr. said [in November 1999] as he introduced legislation for a study of Internet voting. "I believe the Internet could make voting easier, more convenient and extremely efficient."

One might wonder which "community activities" preclude taking an hour or two—out of one day a year—to go and vote. Nevertheless, says Jackson, online voting "presents a fantastic opportunity to reverse a 40-year decline in national voter turnout."

Dick Morris, the brilliant former pollster who worked for any politician whose check cleared, has written a new book, *Vote.com* (a cookbook in the *Twilight Zone* sense, if ever there was one). In *Vote.com*, which is really a piece of promotional literature for his website of the same name, Morris calls for a national system of, at first, "virtual" online plebiscites, from which he plans to make millions. Eventually, he predicts and hopes, the nation will move to the real thing.

He's not the only one. Companies that run secure online elections are proliferating. Dell Computer hyped a recent survey that revealed that almost 80 percent of web users would like to vote online.

So what's wrong with letting people vote when and how they want? Well, everything.

The Dangers of "Pure" Democracy

It's remarkable that just as it is finally dawning on Americans that opinion polls are pernicious, we are moving toward a system that would accentuate the worst aspects of government by poll. Morris writes that the Internet will fulfill Jefferson's vision of direct democracy. He breathlessly endorses Internet referenda in which millions of angry Americans will command politicians to do their bidding on particular issues. Lost on Morris, Ross Perot, and countless other advocates is that Jefferson's vision was rejected by the Founding Fathers, and for very good reason.

In Federalist Number 63, Madison wrote that there are times "when the people, stimulated by some irregular passion may call for measures which they themselves will afterwards be the most ready to lament and condemn. In these critical moments, how salutary will be the interference of some temperate and respectable body of citizens in order to suspend the blow meditated by the people against themselves, until reason, justice, and truth can regain their authority" in public deliberations.

In today's carnival of round-the-clock TV screaming and instant outrage, this concern is even more relevant than it was in Madison's day. Imagine the ill-conceived, MSNBC-inspired legislation that might result from another Oklahoma City bombing. Worse, imagine the incentives for activists and terrorists to stage disasters, if instant democracy were in place.

The Founders rejected a "pure" democracy, in which citizens would run the government in person, because it was obvious to them that such a system would be a petri dish for the bacillus of tyranny. But there are more mundane problems with instant referenda. Conservatives have long lamented

> *"There's [a simple] truth that undermines the case for e-voting: It's too easy."*

that the problem with old, functioning institutions is that people forget why they work. Social planners come along, thinking they can improve schools, families, etc., even though they are entirely ignorant of the thinking that went into creating these institutions in the first place.

An election day, for example, is a vital tool for candidates and voters alike. Informed voters focus their judgments only in the final days of a campaign. Candidates—and journalists—know this. To overturn this system would have unpredictable consequences. It might even place in doubt the very notion of a "mandate"—if a candidate "modified" his position after many votes were cast, but before the actual deadline.

Still, there's an even simpler truth that undermines the case for e-voting: It's too easy. Motor-voter supporters, and others who bemoan low turnout, have never satisfactorily addressed a fundamental question: Why should we care that people who don't care enough to vote aren't voting?

A 1995 poll found that 44 percent of the public thinks that "white males" qualify for preferences under federal affirmative-action programs. These people might indeed vote, if they could do it during a commercial break. Dick Morris and Jesse Jackson Jr. think that would be great. Morris clearly thinks we should listen to these people on issues such as Medicare reform or the WTO.

For good or ill, the deliberative mechanisms of our Constitution have been greatly diminished over the past century. Internet voting would further erode the deliberative process.

The Importance of the Electoral College

Worse still, if the e-rage continues unabated, we can kiss the Electoral College goodbye. Liberals have been itching to kill it for years; an American Bar Association panel concluded in 1969 that this method of electing a president is "archaic, undemocratic, complex, ambiguous, indirect, and dangerous." If independent and third-party voting continues to rise, anti-Electoral College sentiment will surely rise with it. Moreover, if Dick Morris's plebiscitary democracy comes to fruition, old-fashioned state-by-state electioneering will be a forgotten fossil. Instant voters will realize they have more affinity with chatroom buddies a thousand miles away than with the family next door. Combined, all these factors would probably provide the last shove needed to push the Electoral College off the cliff.

You might well ask, So what? But think of what would replace it. State-by-state campaigning is one of the few factors that broaden the issues addressed by our politics. It's an important force in inhibiting the Balkanization of America. [*Balkanization* is a term for geopolitical fragmentation, in reference to the small-scape independence movements that emerged in the Balkan region of Europe at the end of the Cold War.] If we let go of it, politics will become even more dominated by interest groups.

The writing on the wall can be found in a website called "Majority 2000: Women Count." On March 1, 2000, it will hold a women's primary for president, intended to influence many state primaries over the following two weeks. The results of this ballot will be noisily proclaimed by feminists on the cable networks and in other media.

Is it so hard to imagine the next step-binding primaries based on ethnic, sexual, or religious qualifications? For many in the Democratic party, a "Gay Primary" or a "Labor Primary" would be a dream come true. And even for some Republicans—the Christian Coalition comes to mind—a similar system might have some appeal.

History glistens with wonderful gadgets we wouldn't want to be without. None of them came without a price. The Internet, too, will have its downsides. But it will be a shame if one of them is the loss of the very system that made its creation possible.

Media Conglomerates May Dominate the Information Age

by Lawrence Lessig

About the author: *Lawrence Lessig is a law professor at Stanford University and author of* The Future of Ideas: The Fate of the Commons in the Connected World *and* Code and Other Laws of Cyberspace.

Editor's Note: The following viewpoint was written in response to America Online's January 2000 announcement of its plans to merge with fellow media giant Time Warner. The Federal Communications Commission approved the merger in January 2001.

America Online is America's largest Internet service provider. Twenty-two million members get to the Internet through AOL. If it were a state, AOL would rank second in the nation in population, behind California. The company has a market capitalization of $125 billion—a bit less than the Gross Domestic Product (GDP) of Denmark. And with its proposed purchase of one of the largest and most powerful media giants, Time Warner, many are beginning to ask, Should we worry about AOL the way the government worries about Microsoft?

Maybe. But to see why, we've got to look at something politicians don't talk about much—architecture.

At the core of the Internet is a principle of design described by network architects Jerome Saltzer, David P. Reed and David Clark as "end-to-end." The principle of e2e says, Keep the network simple, and build intelligence in the applications ("ends"). Simple networks, smart applications—this was the design choice of the Internet's founders.

The reason was innovation. Simple networks can't discriminate; they are inherently neutral among network uses. Innovators thus don't need to negotiate with every network owner before a new technology is available to all. The burden on innovation is kept small; innovation is, in turn, large.

AOL has benefited from this neutrality. Because regulators breaking up AT&T forced the telephone company to respect e2e neutrality, consumers of telephone service have always had the right to choose the Internet service provider (ISP) they want, not the ISP the telephone company is pushing. This built an architecture of extraordinary competition among ISPs. AOL, by delivering what consumers want, has prevailed in this competition.

All this may change, however, as Internet access moves from narrowband (telephones) to broadband (predominantly cable). Cable companies are not required to respect e2e; they are allowed to discriminate. Unlike telephone companies, they get to choose which "new ideas" will run on cable's network. They get to block services they don't like. Already many

> *"The Microsoft case was about the platform of the 1990s— Windows. The risk that AOL presents is to the platform of the 21st century—the Internet."*

limit the streaming of video to computers (while charging a premium for streaming video to televisions). And this is only the beginning. The list of blocked uses is large and growing.

This trend worries many. AOL fought restrictions when AT&T (after buying a gaggle of cable monopolies) proposed them. But now AOL, by buying Time Warner, is buying its own cable monopolies. And many are worried that AOL will forget its roots. Will the temptation to build its broadband network to protect itself against unallied content and new innovation be too great? Will AOL, like every other large-scale network that has controlled content and conduit, pick a closed rather than an open architecture? Will AOL become what it eats?

Compromising on the principle of e2e would weaken the Internet. It would increase the costs of innovation. If to deploy a new technology or the next killer application—like the World Wide Web was in the early 1990s or gadgets to link the home to the Net may someday become—you first have to negotiate with every cable interest or with every AOL, then fewer innovations will be made. The Internet will calcify to support present-day uses—which is great for the monopolies of today but terrible for the future that the Internet could be.

An analogous issue is at stake in the government's case against Microsoft.* Microsoft argues that it has furthered innovation by providing a platform upon which many application developers have been able to write code. No doubt it has—generally. But the government attacked cases where Microsoft used its power over the platform to stifle technologies that threatened Microsoft's monopoly. The charge was that Microsoft's strategic behavior undermined in-

---

*In May 1998 the U.S. Justice Department filed an antitrust suit against Microsoft, accusing the software giant of abusing its market power to thwart competition. A federal judge ordered in June 2000 that Microsoft be broken up into two companies, but that decision was reversed in 2001.

novation that was inconsistent with Microsoft's business.

The Microsoft case was about the platform of the 1990s—Windows. The risk that AOL presents is to the platform of the 21st century—the Internet. In both cases, the question is whether a strategic actor can chill innovation. With the Internet, that answer depends upon the principles built into the Net.

AOL promises it will behave. It has been a strong defender of "open access" in the past. But its promises are not binding, its slowness in allowing other instant-messaging services onto its platform is troubling, and last month's [May 2000] squabble over access to ABC on Time Warner's network is positively chilling. These are not signs that the principle that built the Internet thrives.

The test will be whether AOL sticks to the principle of e2e, and if it doesn't, whether the government will understand enough to defend the principle in response. If AOL respects e2e in broadband, if it keeps the platform of the network neutral among new uses, if it builds a guarantee into its architecture that innovation will be allowed and encouraged, then we should not worry so much about what AOL owns. Only when it tries to own (through architecture) the right to innovate should we worry.

Sustaining a neutral platform for innovation will be the challenge of the next quarter-century. The danger is the view—common among politicians—that this neutrality takes care of itself. But we have never seen the owners of a large-scale network voluntarily choose to keep it open and free; we should not expect such altruism now. The Internet has taught us the value of such a network. But the government should not be shy to make sure we don't forget it.

The Internet Will Become a More Useful Part of Everyday Life

by **Mark Frauenfelder**

About the author: *Mark Frauenfelder has written articles on technology for the* New York Times Magazine, MIT Technology Review, Yahoo Internet Life, *and the* Industry Standard. *He is also the founding editor in chief of* Wired Online.

How do you endow the Internet's chaotic pile of bits with a structure that makes information easier to find and use? It's all a matter of semantics.

Tim Berners-Lee must feel like he's in a time warp. In the early 1990s, he spent a frustrating year trying to get people to grasp the power and beauty of his idea for a scheme known as an Internet hypertext system, to which he gave the beguiling name the World Wide Web. But since the Web didn't yet exist, most people couldn't imagine the implications of what he was talking about. Berners-Lee persevered, and with the help of the few people who shared his vision, his invention became the fastest-growing media distribution system in history.

A decade later, Berners-Lee is struggling with the same problem—only this time, he's trying to articulate his dream of a Semantic Web. The idea is to weave a Web that not only links documents to each other but also recognizes the meaning of the information in those documents—a task that people can ordinarily do quite well but is a tall order for computers, which can't tell if "head" means the leader of an organization or the thing on top of a body. "The Semantic Web is really data that is processable by machine," says Berners-Lee, who is director of the MIT-based World Wide Web Consortium. "That's what the fuss is about."

Today's World Wide Web is fundamentally a publishing medium—a place to store and share images and text. Adding semantics will radically change the nature of the Web—from a place where information is merely displayed to one where it is interpreted, exchanged and processed. Semantic-enabled search agents will be able to collect machine-readable data from diverse sources, process it and infer new facts. Programs that weren't made to be compatible with each other will share previously unmixable data. In other words, the ultimate goal of the Semantic Web is to give users near omniscience over the vast resources of the Internet, turning the millions of existing database islands into a single gigantic database Pangea.

To compare the Semantic Web with today's Web, Berners-Lee—an intense person who speaks in low-volume bursts—offers the following scenario: Imagine registering for a conference online.

The conference Web site lists the event time, date and location, along with information about the nearest airport and a hotel that offers attendees a discount. With today's Web, you have to first check to make sure your schedule is clear, and if it is you have to cut and paste the time and date into your calendar program. Then you need to make flight and hotel arrangements, either by calling reservations desks, or by going to their Web sites.

"There's no way you can just say, 'I want to go to that event,'" explains Berners-Lee, "because the semantics of which bit is the date and which bit is the time has been lost." But on the Semantic Web, he asserts, those bits will be labeled; the software on your computer will recognize those labels and automatically book your flight to the conference and reserve a hotel room with the click of a button.

The Semantic Web will also be a richer, more customizable Web. Imagine running your cursor over the name of the hotel and being informed that 15 percent of the people who've voted on its quality say it's excellent. If you happen to know that the hotel is a dump, you can instruct your browser to assign those people a trust level of zero. (The polling information would be saved on a third-party "annotation server" that your Web browser accessed automatically.) By assigning high levels of trust to people who match your tastes and interests, and "bozo-filtering" the people who don't, the Web will start looking more like your Web.

It's an enormous undertaking. The first step is to establish standards that allow users to add explicit descriptive tags, or metadata, to Web content— making it easy to pinpoint exactly what you're looking for. Next comes developing methods that enable different programs to relate and share metadata from different Web sites. After that, people can begin crafting additional features, like applications that infer additional facts from the ones they're given. As a result, searches will be more accurate and thorough, data entry will be streamlined and the truthfulness of information will be easier to verify. At least that's the goal.

> *"Adding semantics will radically change the nature of the Web—from a place where information is merely displayed to one where it is interpreted, exchanged and processed."*

Many feel it can't be done. Even though things are heating up in research labs, the Semantic Web as envisioned by Berners-Lee is hampered by social and technical challenges that some critics say may never be solved. But that's not stopping the World Wide Web Consortium and other organizations from trying. The U.S. Defense Advanced Research Projects Agency (DARPA) and commercial enterprises such as Network Inference in Manchester, England, are already developing tools for building the Semantic Web infrastructure—as well as applications for using it. And according to Berners-Lee, with growing numbers of people beginning to grasp how the Semantic Web will "allow more and more sophisticated agents to do things on their behalf," we'll soon see some glimmers of what could be in store.

Untangling the Semantic Web

In his crowded office on the third floor of MIT's Laboratory for Computer Science building, research scientist Eric Miller doesn't seem bothered by the pounding and grinding noises coming from heavy equipment on the construction site next door. As the head of the Semantic Web project, the friendly and energetic Miller is too enthralled with his new job to notice. "I'm the luckiest guy alive," he says. "I get paid for what I'd do for free."

Berners-Lee tapped Miller to head up the consortium's Semantic Web Activity because of Miller's involvement in Web-based knowledge management projects and his ability to

> *"The Semantic Web will ... be a richer, more customizable Web."*

enthusiastically articulate the concepts behind the Semantic Web. Standing next to a whiteboard covered in diagrams of metadata in action, Miller explains that the fundamental idea behind the Semantic Web is to make the Internet more useful to people by making the information floating all over the Web more easily manipulated by computers.

Today, by contrast, most content is formatted for human consumption. When you read a news article online, for instance, you can easily pick out the headline, byline, dateline, photo credit and so on. But unless these things are explicitly labeled, a computer has no idea what they are. It simply sees a bunch of text. In the Semantic Web, a news story will be marked with labels that describe its various parts, making it easy, among other things, for a search engine to find articles written by Jimmy Carter and not stories written about him.

That's not possible today, at least not on a global scale. The formatting tags used to create Web pages are part of the hypertext markup language (HTML), and they describe only what a Web page's information looks like (boldface, small, large, underlined, etc.). The Semantic Web would go beyond cosmetics by including tags that also describe what the information is: tags would label text as designating, for instance, subject, author, street address, price or shipping charge. These descriptive tags are the metadata—the data about the data.

Metadata is not a new concept, nor one restricted to the Internet. A library's card catalogue—with its records describing a book's title, author, subject, year and location on the shelves—is metadata.

The Web made it trivially easy to exchange documents between previously incompatible computers (a few of today's Web users may recall the headaches of the 1980s, when computers from different makers were electronic islands). The Semantic Web will take this a step further, making it possible for computers to exchange particular pieces of information from within documents.

Beyond Metadata

You can't have a Semantic Web without metadata, but metadata alone won't suffice. The metadata in Web pages will have to be linked to special documents that define metadata terms and the relationships between the terms. These sets of shared concepts and their interconnections are called "ontologies."

Say, for example, that you've made a Web page listing the members of a faculty. You would tag the names of the different members with metadata terms such as "chair," "associate professor," "professor" and so on. Then you'd link the page to an ontology—one that you created yourself or one that someone else has already made—that defines educational job positions and how they relate to each other. An appropriate ontology would in this case define a chair as a person, not a thing you sit on, and it would indicate that a chair is the most senior position in a department.

By defining the relationships between terms, ontologies can then be used by applications to infer new facts. Suppose you have created a Web page that teaches schoolchildren about condors, and have added metadata to the content. You could link to an ontology (or more likely, several ontologies) that define the various terms and their relationships: "California condor is a type of condor from California." "Condor is a member of the raptor family." "All raptors are carnivores." "California is a state in the United States." "Carnivores are meat eaters." By using both metadata and ontologies, a search engine or other software agent could find your condor site based on a search request for "carnivores in the U.S?"—even if your site made no mention of carnivores or the United States.

Because ontology development is a big undertaking, it's likely that site creators will link to third-party ontologies. Some will be free, others will be sold or licensed. One issue that will have to be confronted: just as with dictionaries and atlases, political and cultural bias will creep into ontologies. A geography-based ontology maintained by the Chinese government, for instance, would probably not define Taiwan as a "country."

But that hardly impedes the vision. As the World Wide Web Consortium continues to develop standards and technologies for the Semantic Web, hundreds of organizations, companies and individuals are contributing to the effort by creating tools, languages and ontologies.

One major contributor is DARPA—the folks responsible for a great deal of the technology behind the Internet. These days, DARPA is contributing tens of millions of dollars to the Web consortium's Semantic Web project and has developed a semantic language for the U.S. Department of Defense called DARPA Agent Markup Language that allows users to add metadata to Web documents and relate it to ontologies. University of Maryland computer science professor Jim Hendler—who was until August manager of the DARPA program—has been working closely with Berners-Lee and Miller to ensure consistency with the consortium's efforts. [In December 2000], Hendler announced the creation of a language that combines the DARPA Agent Markup Language's capabilities with an ontology language, developed in Europe, called OIL (which stands for both Ontology Inference Layer and Ontology Interchange Language).

> *"Hundreds of organizations, companies and individuals are contributing to the [development of the Semantic Web]."*

A developer of this new language, University of Manchester lecturer Ian Horrocks, also advises the World Wide Web Consortium on the Semantic Web. In January 2001, he cofounded a company called Network Inference to develop technology that uses ontologies and automated inference to give Semantic Web capabilities to existing relational databases and large Web sites. Recently, an Isle of Man–based data services company called PDMS began using Network Inference's technology to add Semantic Web capabilities to corporate databases. Dozens of other companies, from Hewlett-Packard to Nokia, are contributing to Semantic Web development.

Too Much, Too Late?

Miller believes the seamless flow and integration of information resulting from these moves will make it possible to process knowledge in a way "that solves problems, brings people closer and spurs on new ideas that never could happen before." Others, though, are not so optimistic about the Semantic Web. "It's rather ambitious," says R.V. Guha, who led development of the Web consortium's Resource Description Framework efforts in the late 1990s. (This framework is an essential tool for describing and sharing metadata.) "It would be nice if such things existed," he says, "but there are some really hard research problems that need to be solved first."

One issue concerns inference. The time it takes a computer to draw new conclusions from data, metadata and ontologies on the Web increases rapidly as rules are added to a system. Inference falls into the same category as the classic "traveling-salesman problem" of planning the shortest route through a number of cities. It's not hard to figure out the best of all possible routes when you're dealing with just a very few locations. But when you get up to only 15 cities, there are more than 43 billion possible routes. The same kind of runaway situation exists for inference, where brute-force searches for answers could lead to time-wasting paradoxes or contradictions.

And even if Berners-Lee and his cohorts meet the technical challenges, that won't be enough for the Semantic Web to click into place. There is a big question as to whether people will think the benefits are worth the extra effort of adding metadata to their content in the first place. One reason the Web became so wildly successful, after all, was its sublime ease of creation.

"The Web today is the simplest, most primitive form of hypertext," says former Sun Microsystems Distinguished Engineer Jakob Nielsen, cofounder of the Nielsen Norman Group, a Web design firm in Fremont, CA. "And that's why it was so easy to implement; that's why everybody could . . . start putting up their own Web pages; that's why the Web is so big." However, while most people may be comfortable doing simplistic editing, such as marking a text as "bold," Nielsen points out, "They cannot do semantic editing, where they say, 'This is the author's name,' or 'This is the name of people I'm quoting.'"

Of course, such pessimism may be ignoring recent history. Not so long ago, the notion of millions of people learning to write HTML code seemed farfetched—yet that's exactly what happened. Still, the hurdle of creating a Semantic Web will be higher. People can use HTML any way they want. They commonly use tables for nontabular purposes, for instance, and slap on the "subhead" tag merely to apply boldface. These kluges and shortcuts usually have only cosmetic consequences. But the same type of fudging—say, by employing "bibliography" tags to list a DVD collection—could make a page's metadata unusable.

> *"Even though the Semantic Web still resides chiefly on the drawing board, you can see hints of its power on some existing Web sites."*

The fact that metadata wasn't implemented right from the Web's start could also make it harder for the Semantic Web to gain acceptance. One particularly tough skeptic is Peter Merholz, cofounder of Adaptive Path, a San Francisco–based user experience consultancy. "This stuff has to be baked in from the beginning," says Merholz, who calls the Semantic Web "an interesting academic pursuit" with little bearing on society. "The Semantic Web is getting a lot of hype simply because Tim Berners-Lee—the inventor of the World Wide Web—is so interested in it," he says. "If it were just some schmuck at some university in Indiana, nobody would care."

Initial Threads

Even Berners-Lee admits that the path to the Semantic Web may be a bit slower than that to the World Wide Web. "In a way we don't need to move too fast," he says, "because the theory people need to look at it to make sure we're not too crazy, and other people need to check out the ideas in practice before they're picked up and used too extensively."

When asked to peek into his crystal ball, the evangelist of exchangeable data predicts that some of the Semantic Web's first commercial applications will aim to integrate the different information systems that typically coexist in large organizations. (Wouldn't it be nice to take care of business at the motor vehicle department or hospital without having to fill out a half-dozen largely redundant forms? The Semantic Web can help here.)

And even though the Semantic Web still resides chiefly on the drawing board, you can see hints of its power on some existing Web sites. Consider Moreover Technologies' search engine that crawls thousands of news sites several times a day, making it a favorite for news junkies. Moreover's software agents have been programmed to look at the font tags (the HTML labels that tell Web browsers how large or small to make the text appear on the screen) to determine whether or not a particular page is a news story. If a Moreover agent finds a string of six to 18 words tagged as large type near the top of a page, it will assume it is a headline and place it in a database. Of course, since the agent is only making a guess, sometimes it selects a page that isn't news after all. So Moreover has to apply additional filtering to get rid of pages that don't contain articles.

That's still a far cry from the ultimate goal—but it's a good start. And even the Semantic Web champions don't pretend to grasp exactly where such steps will lead. After all, who predicted Amazon.com or eBay back when Berners-Lee turned on the switch of the world's first Web server in December 1990?

But the point is that people want more intelligence from the Web than they're getting—and a growing number of computer scientists share the twinkle in Berners-Lee's eye, and the feeling that the Semantic Web holds the answer. "It's great," says the inventor of the World Wide Web, "to have that grass-roots enthusiasm around again."

Society Will Become Increasingly Interconnected in the Information Age

by Tom Regan

About the author: *Tom Regan is a staff writer for the* Christian Science Monitor.

Welcome to the age of online, everywhere, all the time. We are quickly approaching the moment when Internet access will be possible from any point on the planet.

In industrialized nations, that access will become invisible to many people. Networked homes will create a living space where tablet-sized PCs will talk to the fridge, the toaster, even the garbage pail, often when the residents are not home.

For some people, this will be an enormous benefit. Fully wired homes for senior citizens, for instance, will use the Net to help them stay independent far longer than in the past.

These are only a few promises that the Internet holds for us. And even with a downturn in New Economy businesses, countries ignore these developments at their own risk.

Hyper-Connectedness

But while the promise of being constantly connected to the Net may seem desirable to many, it also raises questions about the social consequences of this hyper-connectedness.

Questions such as: What does it mean to be online all the time? How will that change the way we live? What are the benefits and the drawbacks to being constantly connected?

For Adam Clayton Powell III of the Freedom Forum, an international foundation dedicated to free speech, being online all the time means paying more attention to our choices.

"It's easy to say we would just have more of the same: more speed, more multitasking, more frequent messages," Mr. Powell says. "But maybe we will see something more qualitative than quantitative—watch kids doing homework with four or five instant-chat windows open. Is this just more, or is it something very different from, say, sitting quietly with a book? Whatever that difference is, that's what is coming."

For James Adams, head of iDefense, a firm that specializes in global security, "There is a price to be paid for this [ubiquitous] access," he says. "It's a loss of individuality or anonymity. Anytime you ask for or are given something, you will need to provide data about yourself.

"And that data can be used for you or against you. The pace at which this is all unfolding makes it almost impossible for governments, or NGOs [nongovernmental organizations], to plan how to deal with it."

The Haves and the Have-Nots

Dave Allred, vice president of Broadband Services for Telocity, one of America's leading DSL [digital subscriber lines, a type of high-speed Internet connection] firms, sees another problem—equality of access.

"We need to be aware of the digital divide, between Internet haves and have-nots," he says. "If you look at our society, it's becoming a service- and information-oriented culture. Access to information has become a fundamental part of what we do. It can make a real difference at the level of the individual's life."

Perhaps even more interesting will be the way the Internet ultimately empowers the individual to take political or social action. "This revolution—and that's what it is—will give voice to the individual in ways not seen before," Mr. Adams says.

"The question is what will this social activism look like? Will it be using the Internet to write an e-mail to your senator or will it be to operate a social-activist chat room that organizes large online protests against government and corporations?" Adams asks. "I don't think that the nature of this power has been understood by those who have it yet. It may look very much like anarchy, and there is a danger in that, too."

Yet how realistic are these predictions of ubiquitous Internet access? How popular is the Internet?

Recent Yankelovich/Monitor surveys of 857 Internet users in 1999

"What does it mean to be online all the time? How will that change the way we live?"

and 1,039 in 2000 showed a decline in Internet use. The thrust of the study was that people are bored with the Net and spend less time using it.

Yet other studies show dramatically different results. A survey by the Pew Internet and the American Life Project showed that Americans continued to flock online, across all ages and economic groups, growing from 88 million Internet users in May 2000 to more than 104 million by the end of 2000. (More than 4,500 Internet and non-Internet users were interviewed in May and June [2000] and 3,500 in late November and December.)

As for time spent online, the data showed the average dropped by only a few minutes between May and December [2000]. On the other hand, the number of adults using the Net increased 4 percent over the same period, or by about 11 million a day.

> *"Whether we like it or not, the Internet will continue to find its way into our daily routines."*

The legerdemain of Internet statistics is complicated by the fact that the Internet is becoming so woven into our lives—quickly moving beyond the desktop computer—that we may not even notice we're online. Do those who instant message 10 times a day via PCs, cellphones, or PDAs (personal digital assistants) realize they're online?

The GSM Association, which sets wireless communication standards, reported April 5 [2001] that more than 15 billion SMS (short message service) text messages were sent worldwide in December 2000. The group predicts that total will climb to more than 200 billion by the end of 2002.

In short, we've never been more able to reach out and touch each other.

The Holy Grail

These days more businesses use the Internet to conduct key transactions. A recent report by Forrester Research showed that the online wholesale energy trade will reach $3.6 trillion by 2005, saving the industry millions of dollars.

Meanwhile, more homes are turning into small Internet hubs of their own. Cahners In-Stat Group reported that the in-home networking equipment market jumped more than 97 percent last year.

Mr. Allred of Telocity sees a future where every home will have Internet access, regardless of economic factors.

"Some folks will have very simple access to the Internet, while others will have faster connections."

Some families will have fully networked homes. Others will choose a single high-speed connection. Families at the low end of the economic spectrum will have dial-up access. But make no mistake, Allred says, anyone who wants the Internet will have it.

For those who work for Internet businesses, to be online, everywhere, all the time, is the goal of their industry.

"It's constantly on our minds," Allred says. "It is the Holy Grail. We want to get to the point where service, information, and data, in user-friendly ways, are available in all the appropriate devices our customers want them in."

For Bob Metcalfe, the inventor of Ethernet and founder of 3Com, constant access has few downsides. "Nothing bad, as I would have more choices, not less," Mr. Metcalfe said via e-mail. "More communication is better—many problems stem from a failure to communicate. . . . A recent *National Geographic* chart showed the number of languages spoken by humans on earth declining over the ages. . . .

"Some people, especially French-speaking people . . . lament language convergence. I don't. . . . This is part of the inexorable trend toward more-frequent and higher-fidelity communication among us, which I think bodes well for the human race."

The Danger of Being "Always On"

So be aware. Whether we like it or not, the Internet will continue to find its way into our daily routines. In the future, we may even wear our Internet connections.

For many, it's hard to escape feeling slightly uncomfortable with it all.

"The benefit and the danger" of being constantly connected is being constantly accessible, Powell says. "It's not great to be overwhelmed by hundreds of incoming messages." At the recent New Mexico Media Forum in Taos, Powell says, he was interested by the reaction of participants when they realized their pagers and cellphones didn't work there: "Most cheered."

There Will Be a Backlash Against the Information Age

by Karl Albrecht and Ronald Gunn

About the authors: *Karl Albrecht is chairman of Karl Albrecht International, a business consulting firm in San Diego, and author of more than twenty books on management and organizational effectiveness. Ronald Gunn is managing director of Strategic Futures Consulting Group in Alexandria, Virginia.*

Something strange happened on January 1, 2000: All across America and the rest of the developed world, nothing strange happened.

Virtually everybody was keyed up for the dreaded Y2K event (which meant little more to most people than the turnover of computer clocks), but what we got was a nonevent. No economic meltdown, no financial disasters, no planes falling from the sky, no food riots. The anarchists and doomsday cults also came up empty. It was, by any measure, a Big Letdown. Many people seemed disappointed when nothing happened. It was as if a long-awaited party had been canceled, without explanation.

The arrival of the Digital Millennium seems to have depressed many of us. What otherwise should have been a time for each person to celebrate, ruminate, appreciate, take stock, reflect, dream, and enjoy turned out to be a botched exercise in Digital Mania.

We assert that many people, perhaps a sizable majority, felt vaguely cheated. Yes, there were parties; yes, the ball dropped in Times Square; yes, the news magazines conducted the obligatory review of the century. But, for many people, it all added up to a hollow exercise without the deep personal meaning they had expected (perhaps unconsciously) to feel. We were robbed of a personal milestone and left vaguely dissatisfied.

Digital Angst

Many people are still experiencing Digital Angst. If the economy is booming, why doesn't business seem to be fun anymore? Could it be that the triumph of digital process over imaginative substance is wearing thin? Could there be nascent discomfort with the increasingly apparent power imbalance between humans and technology? Why do so many of us feel that we're on a treadmill to nowhere? Who—or what—are we supposed to be keeping up with? And aren't we all just a little tired of hearing about the Internet?

Instant, mostly young, dot.com millionaires are the new heroes of American culture. News reports of their huge success seem to be from another world—the world across the Digital Divide. The dramatic stories on CNN and from other business media contribute to a win-lose, heroes-failures psychosis. As in the Roman gladiator contests, you're either a winner or you're dead.

The big surprise of the Digital Divide may be that it's rapidly becoming more ideological and psychosocial than economic and technical.

In recent years, the Internet and all things digital have outranked almost every other story in news broadcasts, books, and magazine articles. Journalists (wittingly or not) have united with makers of computers and software and with Internet service providers in a half-conscious collusion to popularize the Net phenomenon. The gee-whiz technocracy, with the popular press waving the banner, has an almost messianic obsession with selling the benefits of digital technology to T.C. Mits and T.C. Wits (the celebrated man and woman in the street). We feel it's proper to ask whether the fascination with digital gadgetry, especially in America, is the subject of or result of the unprecedented media treatment.

In its earliest days, Internet devotees hailed it as "the great democratizer." It would level the effects of social status, economic conditions, and political clout. It would put even the tiniest businesses on the same footing with the mighty giants. Now, even the Internet's most rabid promoters concede that it is having the opposite effect. It exaggerates the disparity between the haves and the have-nots. Notwithstanding politically correct ads showing adorable black children somewhere in Africa logging on to the Web, poor people won't be lifted out of their dire economic circumstances by computers or the Internet.

> *"Aren't we all just a little tired of hearing about the Internet?"*

An unvoiced assumption seems to be that all human beings have an equal appetite for consuming and processing information. That seems questionable, judging by the low sales of nonfiction books, for example. The lack of convergence (as predicted) of television and the Internet also casts doubt on a universal insatiability for information.

Listening to its more vocal and determined advocates, one gets the feeling that the Digital Doctrine takes on an almost Fascist overtone, eerily reminiscent of the political environment in prewar Germany. That may seem extreme, but many well-educated adults have confided to us that they feel intellectually intimidated by what they call the "techno-Nazi" ideology and are reluctant to speak their misgivings. More people, including those who use computers and the Internet regularly, say they are feeling caught in an ideological stampede of sorts.

To read the subtext of the Digital Drama, there's a clearly defined Digital Doctrine—a set of Orwellian ideological premises that must be embraced. What are the key propositions, spoken and unspoken, that define the Digital Doctrine and shape its energy?

The Digital Doctrine

We seem to be expected to believe the following tenets:
- Technology is a thing unto itself, an all-pervasive agent that governs our lives—as opposed to something that people choose to do with gadgets.
- If a thing can be done, then it will be done and, indeed, must be done—for example, connecting your refrigerator to the Internet.
- The Wired World is our destiny. You must learn to love (or at least live with) the Big Brother aspect. Otherwise, you will certainly be left Out (of something) and left behind (somebody).
- Some of us get it, and the ones who don't must either be helped to get it or be driven like sheep to their ultimate destiny to love it in the end.

Vocabulary signals ideology. One of the clearest signs of a developing new ideology is the special lingo its devotees use to signal their allegiance to new truths. Characteristically, the Digital World has cyber-speak, a notably impersonal patois of processes and things. The New Economy-Old Economy shibboleth signals an attitude, a narcissistic in-group psychology that says, "We're the enlightened ones; we get it. Anybody who doesn't agree with the cyber-ideology doesn't get it and will be left behind."

Internet language reflects a pecking order: a newbie is a freshman who is expected to be properly humble and respectful toward those who got there first. Classifications according to technology affinity, such as late adopters and resisters, apply labels to anyone who doesn't enthusiastically embrace a particular new technology.

As management consultants, we've watched with considerable amusement as the "geeks" have suddenly discovered business. In no other dimension of practice have we seen such a rush of idealistic, narcissistic, and ill-informed zealots who have no interest in learning from the experience of others. In record time, the invading cyber-Vikings have created their own business ideology and vocabulary, which, they say, taking great pains to emphasize, owe nothing to the traditional thinking processes of commerce. They characterize established enterprises as "old economy" or "bricks and mortar" to authorize themselves to "reinvent" business. "After all," they pronounce, "the Internet changes everything. The old rules no longer apply"—implying, so why bother to learn them?

Here's a peculiar fact: Many of the Netizens who are promoting the Net and all forms of e-business are the same people who screamed bloody murder in the mid 1990s when America Online announced it would give its customers access to the Internet at no extra charge. They lamented that allowing hordes of civilians onto the Internet would clutter up the place with a bunch of newbies and nuisances.

Actually, the Internet will evolutionize business, but not revolutionize it. In fact, companies that take best advantage of online technology are turning out to be the established leaders in the so-called old economy—retailers, publishers, catalogue marketers, banks, and all the rest. Consider that as early as 1989, Hewlett-Packard decided to wire the entire company, putting more than 90,000 employees in contact with each other. Procter & Gamble and Wal-Mart have linked their computer systems—b2b in the current jargon—for well over a decade.

Ironically, many of the old rules still apply, to the consternation of new-economy entrepreneurs. Mark Twain, arguably one of the best marketing consultants in history, lived during the time of the California gold rush. He advised, "When everybody is out digging for gold, the business to be in is selling shovels." Few independent miners made fortunes digging for gold; most went broke. Selling shovels was indeed more profitable than digging with them. One of the few millionaires to emerge from the gold rush period was a Jewish immigrant named Levi Strauss, who made heavy-duty work clothes out of denim and sold them to miners. The ones going broke on the Internet are those digging for gold; the ones making profits are selling them the shovels.

> *"Many well-educated adults have confided to us that they feel intellectually intimidated by what they call the 'techno-Nazi' ideology."*

In the business sector, Dot.Com Delusion has spawned a whole new set of ethical dilemmas. Entrepreneurs team up with venture capitalists and stock underwriters to launch businesses that have no hope of long-term viability. Investors rush in like eager sheep, part with their fleece, and are left with worthless hides (at least for the purposes of this metaphor) while the insiders walk away with their cash. Almost all of the so-called Internet millionaires are actually stock market millionaires. It has been about market valuation, not value in the marketplace.

The new message to young people thinking about starting a business is, "Forget built to last and learn built to flip." More companies are being created with the sole purpose of taking them public and then flipping them. The quaint idea of building a going concern that will deliver long-term shareholder value is nowhere in the equation. The new cyber-hero isn't the entrepreneur who works hard to build a viable firm, but the one clever enough to promote it and flip it, moving on to the next one before the bills come due. Established firms are, in many cases, at a disadvantage vis-a-vis unprofitable digital-mania firms that can use hyper-inflated share prices to acquire other firms without putting up cash. That puts enormous pressure on executives of all firms to use PR gimmicks and accounting tricks to try to boost share prices to unsustainable levels. Unabated, snake oil begets more snake oil.

A Few Predictions

E-commerce will be the big failure story of the decade. Successful companies will, of course, continue to use online technology to simplify and integrate their operations, interlocking their systems more with those of suppliers and partners. And most established companies will extend their market reach through Web technology. However, the heart of the e-commerce story as promoted by the press, namely the Internet-only company, will eventually be seen as a total failure.

Internet-only companies doomed themselves to unprofitability early by adopting a fanatical giveaway mentality. The idea was to forget about actually selling anything on your Website (at least not for a profit margin) and just get as many people as you can to visit your site—in other words, to aggregate eyeballs. When people visit your site, you can sell their names to other e-merchants that want to advertise their products. Only a few firms have made that portal approach work, and they get most of their revenue from the many smaller Web wannabes that spend their investors' capital trying to build attention share. Few Internet-only companies actually sell enough of anything to cover their advertising and operating costs. As they go out of business and stop buying advertising, even the major portals may go out with them.

Internet companies have been burning through investor capital at an alarming rate, and few have shown enough sales productivity to justify further investment. Despite the breathless press stories about the phenomenal growth rate of online commerce—in percentage terms, of course—the fact is that online sales account for only a small fraction of total retail sales, even in America.

The enormous promotional investment fueling the current level of attention to, interest in, and economic activity surrounding everything digital can't be sustained indefinitely. As Internet businesses fail in droves and the investments fail to perform as hoped, digital capital will be scarcer and the artificially sustained energy will wane. Once the Net-bubble has deflated, there will be a massive sag in energy and money for all things digital. Internet Fatigue, as we call it, will be signaled by the widely expressed attitude: "We're tired of hearing about the Internet."

> *"E-commerce will be the big failure story of the decade."*

Fundamental to the Digital Doctrine is the sacred principle that the number of Internet users will grow without bounds, eventually including all but about three people on the planet. MIT's director of media technology, Nicholas Negroponte, predicted in 1997 that "there will be 1 billion people on the Internet by the year 2000." Many "by the year 2000" predictions are becoming an embarrassment now that 2000 has arrived. Nothing rises to the sky, and pundits who don't understand the principle of the S-curve get to learn about it in a practical way.

The S-curve is a natural principle, almost on a par with gravity, that dictates patterns of growth for everything from bacteria colonies to human populations to stock prices to market demand for new products. Any fast-rising variable goes through an early "getting started" phase, followed by a sharp upward acceleration and then a slower rate of growth that may level off. Plotted on a chart, the pattern looks like a stretched letter S, with its overall shape determined by the rate of growth and distance

> *"What if not everyone is yearning to be a cyber-citizen?"*

from the foot to the shoulder. There's every reason to believe that the number of Internet users will also follow the S-curve.

As for 1 billion people on the Internet, we ask, Really? All with more than $10 dollars to spend per year? What if the eventual Internet population isn't 99 percent of the developed world? Suppose it turns out to be less than half, regardless of economics or education, because of people's individual mental proclivity? It seems clear that, even in a highly educated population, some people are more information-oriented than others. What if not everyone is yearning to be a cyber-citizen?

Where might we be on the S-curve now? Most dot.com business models, and much of the economic ideology of the Digital Agenda, assume we're on the early rising part of the S. A frightening thought: What if we're much farther up the S-curve than most people think? What if the hard core of addictive users is mostly committed to the Internet and the rest of us can take it or leave it? How many ventures hang on the assumption of continued exponential growth?

Consider that two-thirds of the world population has never heard a dial tone. Nearly half has no reliable access to electricity or running water. In all likelihood, not more than 10 percent will be eligible economically for the Internet within the next 20 years. The idea that all we have to do is give people computers is a projection of a distinctly American, upper-middle-class worldview and smacks of the Great Society. It's the cyber-equivalent of "Let them eat cake."

In America, home of the first and most wired population on the planet, it seems likely that more than half of the people who will use the Internet in anything more than an occasional way are already doing so. Will every new gadget and killer application grow the population of Internet users, eventually recruiting everyone? That seems more and more unlikely.

Internet Fatigue is already in evidence. The scenario, as we see it: As the Dot.Com Death March continues, more investors will lose faith in the Internet Fantasy. The Digital Dream will become the Digital Nightmare. The same herd of investors who rushed in will rush out of Internet-based stocks—and possibly the whole category, but certainly away from the gee-whiz sectors. Venture capitalists will become choosier and will gravitate toward the shovel makers. At the same time, established "old economy" firms will become ever more competent and aggressive at extending their businesses with online technology.

Profit margins and earnings growth rates of even the most worshipped online companies, such as America Online, will remain appallingly low, and their share prices will be brutally repriced to normal levels. We will likely see one or more major icons of e-commerce such as Amazon.com fail or have to be acquired to continue operating. Advertising expenditures will fall precipitously as venture capital dries up and dot.bomb companies trying to survive cut budgets and promote themselves with Internet banner ads, merely prolonging their agony. Few portals, if any, will stay profitable.

Ironically, there will be a dramatic return of attention in business (and by CNN) to the so-called old-economy companies—you remember, the ones with actual profits. CNN and other media will, of course, claim that they knew all along that the dot.com boom couldn't last.

The ultimate expression of Internet Fatigue will be a loss of interest—a Digital Depression. It won't be possible for the media to keep up the drama indefinitely. Even people who use PC-Net technology every day will be saying, "Enough, already. I get it. The Internet is here. Now, let's get on with our lives." The hard-core addicted population of about 15 to 20 million people worldwide will continue to live in the Wired World. Meanwhile, the digital middle class will continue to take it or leave it.

Digital Deliverance

Once we've wired the world, we can't unwire it. Is that what we want? If we assume that the wiring will continue at breakneck speed, what are the consequences of not forging a balance between humans and technology? The sci-fi-like scenarios of artificial intelligence surpassing human intelligence take on a meaning with greater gravitas: If we don't insist on substance first, served by process second, and we fail to re-emphasize that technology exists to serve the aims of human community, then a quiet new elite may emerge: people who can turn off the TV and the PC and think.

After one of our recent talks, a senior executive mused, "You know, there'll come a day when people will pay a lot of money to go where they can't be connected."

Organizations to Contact

The editors have compiled the following list of organizations concerned with the issues debated in this book. The descriptions are derived from materials provided by the organizations. All have publications or information available for interested readers. The list was compiled on the date of publication of the present volume; the information provided here may change. Be aware that many organizations take several weeks or longer to respond to inquiries, so allow as much time as possible.

American Library Association (ALA)
50 E. Huron, Chicago, IL 60611
(800) 545-2433
website: www.ala.org

A trade organization representing America's librarians, the ALA provides leadership for the development, promotion, and improvement of library and information services and the profession of librarianship. The ALA supports free access to library materials and resources and opposes the Children's Online Protection Act, which requires public libraries to install content filtering software on computers with Internet access. The ALA publishes the magazine *American Libraries* and the *Newsletter on Intellectual Freedom*.

Americans for Computer Privacy (ACP)
website: www.computerprivacy.org

ACP is a broad-based coalition that brings together more than one hundred companies and forty associations representing financial services, manufacturing, telecommunications, high-tech, and transportation, as well as law enforcement, civil-liberty, pro-family, and taxpayer groups. ACP supports policies that advance the rights of American citizens to encode information without fear of government intrusion and opposes government efforts to increase widespread monitoring or surveillance. The organization publishes news alerts and issue overviews on its website.

Bridges.org
1424 16th St. NW, Suite 502, Washington, DC 20036
(202) 299-0120
website: www.bridges.org

Bridges.org is an international nonprofit organization that works to help span the digital divide. Bridges.org researches, tests, and promotes best practices for sustainable, empowering use of information and communication technology. The organization publishes reports, research, and position papers.

Center for Democracy and Technology (CDT)
1634 Eye St. NW, Suite 1100, Washington, DC 20006
(202) 637-9800
website: www.cdt.org

CDT's mission is to develop public policy solutions that advance constitutional civil liberties and democratic values in the new computer and communications media. Pursuing its mission through policy research, public education, and coalition building, the center works to increase citizens' privacy and the public's control over the use of personal information held by government and other institutions. Its publications include the reports *Broadband Access: Maximizing the Democratic Potential of the Internet* and *Bridging the Digital Divide: Central & Eastern Europe*, as well as issue briefs and policy papers.

Computer Professionals for Social Responsibility (CPSR)
PO Box 717, Palo Alto, CA 94302
(650) 322-3778
website: www.cpsr.org

CPSR works to provide the public and policy makers with realistic assessments of the power, promise, and problems of information technology. CPSR members work to direct public attention to critical choices concerning the applications of information technology and how those choices affect society. It publishes the quarterly *CPSR Journal* and the *PING!* newsletter.

The Democracy Online Project
The Graduate School of Political Management, George Washington University
805 21st St. NW, Suite 401, Washington, DC 20052
(800) 367-4776
website: www.democracyonline.org

The Democracy Online Project studies the impact of the Internet on politics and promotes fair online campaign practices. Its publications include the report *Digital Donors: How Campaigns Are Using the Internet to Raise Money and How It's Affecting Democracy* and testimonies from the conference "In Search of Democracy's Domain in a Dot-Com World."

Digital Promise Project
c/o The Century Foundation
41 E. 70th St., New York, NY 10021
(212) 535-4441
website: www.digitalpromise.org

Digital Promise's goal is to unlock the potential of the Internet and other new information technologies for education. It funds efforts to train teachers in the use of information technology and to digitize educational resources. The *Digital Promise Report* is available for download on the organization's website.

Electronic Frontier Foundation (EFF)
454 Shotwell St., San Francisco, CA 94110-1914
(415) 436-9333
website: www.eff.org

EFF is an organization of students and other individuals that aims to promote a better understanding of telecommunications issues. It fosters awareness of civil liberties issues arising from advancements in computer-based communications media and supports litigation to preserve, protect, and extend First Amendment rights in computing and Internet technologies. EFF publishes a comprehensive archive of digital civil liberties information on its website.

Electronic Privacy Information Center (EPIC)
1718 Connecticut Ave. NW, Suite 200, Washington, DC 20009
(202) 483-1140
website: www.epic.org

EPIC is a public interest research center that works to focus public attention on emerging civil liberties issues and to protect privacy, the First Amendment, and constitutional values. It supports privacy-protection legislation and provides information on how individuals can protect their online privacy. EPIC publishes the *EPIC Alert* newsletter and the *Privacy Law Sourcebook.*

Enough Is Enough
(888) 2Enough
e-mail: eieca@enough.org • website: www.enough.org

Enough Is Enough is an independent nonprofit organization that works to educate the public and policy makers about the harms of pornography and to protect children from exposure to Internet pornography and online predators. Enough Is Enough publications include a newsletter, the manual *Enough Is Enough "Safe Surfing in the Library,"* and the brochure *Safe Journeys on the Information Superhighway.*

Internet Society
1775 Wiehle Ave., Suite 102, Reston, VA 20190-5108
(703) 326-9880
website: www.isoc.org

A group of technologists, developers, educators, researchers, government representatives, and businesspeople, the Internet Society supports the development and dissemination of standards for the Internet and works to ensure global cooperation and coordination for the Internet and related Internet-working technologies and applications. It publishes the bimonthly magazine *On the Internet.*

World Future Society
7910 Woodmont Ave., Suite 450, Bethesda, MD 20814
(800) 898-8274
website: www.wfs.org

The society is an association of people interested in how social and technological developments are shaping the future. It serves as a clearinghouse for ideas about the future. The WFS publishes the *Futurist,* a bimonthly magazine, and hosts the Cyber Society Forum on its website, where participants submit essays on the future of information technology.

Websites

E-Fairness Coalition
www.e-fairness.org

The coalition represents brick-and-mortar and online retailers, retail corporations and associations, publicly and privately owned shopping centers, outlet centers and independently owned shops, and a total of over 350,000 retail stores nationwide. It opposes special tax exemptions for online business.

Falling Through the Net
www.digitaldivide.gov

This site was established by the Commerce Department's National Telecommunications and Information Administration (NTIA) to inform the public of the federal government's activities regarding Americans' access to the Internet and other information technologies. The site contains the reports *Falling Through the Net: Defining the Digital Divide, Falling Through the Net: Toward Digital Inclusion,* and *A Nation Online: How Americans Are Expanding Their Use of the Internet.*

Bibliography

Books

Cynthia J. Alexander and Leslie A. Pal, eds.
Digital Democracy: Policy and Politics in the Wired World. New York: Oxford University Press, 1998.

Eric Banks
E-Finance: The Electronic Revolution. Chichester, NY: J. Wiley, 2001.

David B. Bolt and Ray A.K. Crawford, eds.
Digital Divide: Computers and Our Children's Future. New York: TV Books, 2000.

Frances Cairncross
The Death of Distance: How the Communications Revolution Is Changing Our Lives. Boston: Harvard Business School Press, 2001.

Martin Carnoy
Sustaining the New Economy: Work, Family, and Community in the Information Age. New York: Russell Sage Foundation, 2000.

Benjamin M. Compaine, ed.
The Digital Divide: Facing a Crisis or Creating a Myth? Cambridge, MA: MIT Press, 2001.

Richard Davis
The Web of Politics: The Internet's Impact on the American Political System. New York: Oxford University Press, 1999.

Bosa Ebo, ed.
Cyberimperialism?: Global Relations in the New Electronic Frontier. Westport, CT: Praeger, 2001.

Simson Garfinkel
Database Nation: The Death of Privacy in the 21st Century. Cambridge, MA: O'Reilly, 2001.

Wendy Grossman
From Anarchy to Power: The Net Comes of Age. New York: New York University Press, 2001.

Charles Jennings et al.
The Hundredth Window: Protecting Your Privacy and Security in the Age of the Internet. New York: Free Press, 2000.

Rosabeth Moss Kanter
Evolve!: Succeeding in the Digital Culture of Tomorrow. Boston: Harvard Business School Press, 2001.

Lawrence Lessig
The Future of Ideas: The Fate of the Commons in a Connected World. New York: Random House, 2001.

Bibliography

Anthony B. Perkins and Michael C. Perkins	*The Internet Bubble: The Inside Story on Why It Burst—and What You Can Do to Profit Now.* New York: HarperBusiness, 2001.
Robert B. Reich	*The Future of Success: Working and Living in the New Economy.* New York: A. Knopf, 2000.
Marc J. Rosenberg	*E-Learning: Strategies for Delivering Knowledge in the Information Age.* New York: McGraw-Hill, 2001.
Andrew L. Shapiro	*The Control Revolution: How the Internet Is Putting Individuals in Charge and Changing the World We Know.* New York: Public Affairs, 1999.
Cass Sunstein	*Republic.com.* Princeton, NJ: Princeton University Press, 2001.
Don Tapscott	*Growing Up Digital: The Rise of the Net Generation.* New York: McGraw-Hill, 1998.
Lester C. Thurow	*Building Wealth: The New Rules for Individuals, Companies, and Nations in a Knowledge-Based Economy.* New York: HarperCollins, 1999.
Jonathan D. Wallace	*Sex, Laws, and Cyberspace: Freedom and Censorship on the Frontiers of the Online Revolution.* New York: M & T Books, 1996.
Anthony G. Wilhelm	*Democracy in the Digital Age: Challenges to Political Life in Cyberspace.* New York: Routledge, 2000.

Periodicals

John Adam	"Internet Everywhere," *Technology Review*, September 2000.
William Beaver	"The Dilemma of Internet Pornography," *Business & Society Review*, Fall 2000.
John Seely Brown	"Growing Up Digital," *Change*, March 2000.
Craig A. Cunningham	"Improving Our Nations' Schools Through Computers & Connectivity," *Brookings Review*, Winter 2001.
Samuel L. Dunn	"The Webcentric University," *Futurist*, July 2001.
Economist	"From Dot.com to Dot.bomb," July 1, 2000.
Economist	"Is There Life in E-Commerce? Is There Life in Internet Commerce?" February 3, 2001.
James Fallows	"Can the Net Govern Itself?" *American Prospect*, March 27, 2000.
Christopher Farrell	"The Case for Optimism," *Business Week*, October 9, 2000.
David Gelernter	"Will We Have Any Privacy Left?" *Time*, February 21, 2000.
George Gilder	"The Coming Boom," *American Spectator*, May 2001.
Joshua Green	"The Online Education Bubble," *American Prospect*, October 23, 2000.

Walter Kirn	"Recession for Dummies: Why the New Economy Went Bust," *Time*, March 5, 2001.
Lawrence Lessig	"Innovation, Regulation, and the Internet," *American Prospect*, March 27, 2000.
Aaron Lukas	"Should Internet Sales Be Taxed?" *USA Today*, January 2001.
Charles C. Mann	"Taming the Web," *Technology Review*, September 2001.
National Journal	"The Virtual Voting Booth," November 4, 2000.
Noam Neusner and Brooke Adams	"Not-So-Great Expectations," *U.S. News & World Report*, April 9, 2001.
Newsweek	"The Web's Dark Secret," March 19, 2001.
Geoffrey Nunberg	"The Internet Filter Farce," *American Prospect*, January 1, 2001.
Ramesh Ponnuru	"The Tax Man Cometh—How Will He Handle the Internet?" *National Review*, June 19, 2000.
Adam Clayton Powell III	"Falling for the Gap," *Reason*, November 1999.
William Safire	"Age of Consent," *New York Times*, March 12, 2001.
Christopher H. Schmitt and Joellen Perry	"World Wide Weapon," *U.S. News & World Report*, November 15, 2001.
Debora Spar	"When the Anarchy Has to Stop," *New Statesman*, October 15, 2001.
Jim Thomas	"Imagining Tomorrow," *USA Today*, July 2001.
Time	"Is the New Economy Dead?" October 23, 2000.
Time	"This Time It's Different," January 8, 2001.
Jonathan D. Wallace	"Preserving Anonymity on the Internet," *USA Today*, November 2000.

Index